Hope & Help *for the* Widow

The Reality *of* Being Alone

Hope & Help
for the & Widow

The Reality of Being Alone

Jan Sheble

PUBLISHED BY
AMG *Publishers*

Hope and Help for the Widow: The Reality of Being Alone

ISBN 0-89957-141-7

First printing—April 2003

Cover designed by ImageWright, Inc., Chattanooga, Tennessee
Interior design and typesetting by Reider Publishing Services, West
    Hollywood, California
Edited and Proofread by Judy Bodmer, Robert Kelly, Dan Penwell, and
    Jody El-Assadi

Printed in the United States of America
09 08 07 06 05 04 03 –P– 8 7 6 5 4 3 2 1

This book is dedicated to the Lord Jesus Christ,
the Great Healer,
who is eager to comfort the widow.

Acknowledgments

I am grateful to:

Dan Penwell and the entire staff of AMG Publishers for their confidence in me and for their encouragement, and

Judy Bodmer, Robert Kelly, and Jody El-Assadi for their nitpicky editing and proofreading, and

Those widows whose lives and stories have inspired me to write this book, and

Jerry Waggoner for his assistance and support as I wrote this book.

Contents

Foreword

Dear Reader,

This is a book I wish I didn't have to write and one I wish you didn't have to read. But the deaths of our husbands have altered our lives. This isn't something any of us signed up for, but, nevertheless, here we are—widows. In this sense, we're of the same family. Our spirits understand one another, as others around us cannot. They offer sincere sympathy, but only one who has walked through that valley herself can truly say, "I understand."

We can't change what's happened. If we truly trust in the sovereignty of God, we acknowledge that he indeed knows what is best. Intellectually we understand that he has ordained all our days (see Ps. 139:16). We know that our God is in control. We are his daughters.

Nevertheless, we are human. We grieve. We hurt. We have anger. We have fears. We need kindred sisters who understand these feelings. Together, we can work our way through them and face tomorrow.

Our task, overwhelming as it may seem, is to share with each other and to draw from each other's strength. As you go through this book, I pray that you will consider me to be one of your kindred sisters. Be assured that although I may not know you, I've been praying for you as the Lord led me to write these words.

I'll share some stories about other widows whom I've given fictitious names. Some of these stories are composites of what I've learned from working with, talking with, and ministering to many others who have been widowed. If anything in these stories reminds you of yourself or someone else, it's coincidental. Frequently, there are similarities in the stories because of the experiences we share as women who have lost a husband. I relate these stories so that you might glean and grow from the experiences of other widows. When I do share in depth from my own personal experiences, it's only to give you a focused insight into my walk through widowhood.

Any recommendations I make in the book are purely ideas I've garnered from studying, reading, and speaking with others. Suggestions, especially in the legal area or of financial concerns, are only my opinion. For expert advice in these or other areas, you should consult professionals in the field.

As widows, we may weep and we may laugh, but we may also still have unresolved issues that trouble us. If you're reading this book on your own, rest in that. I suggest you begin at chapter one and read the chapters consecutively, for they build on one another. Perhaps you're going through this book with a friend. That's okay too. The most important aspect of working your way through this book is that you are doing it.

If you're reading this book as part of a support group or a study class, you'll have others to share with as well. I suggest that you read one chapter per week by yourself. Appendix A lists questions to use during your support group meetings. In Appendix B, you will find guidelines and suggestions on the format and logistics of a support group. To help you stay focused, you may find it helpful to review those guidelines each time the group meets. Appendix C is composed of topical questions and answers as an aid for further reflection. These questions have been answered from personal experiences, interviews, and further research. Some of the answers you will agree with, others you may not, but hopefully, they will make you think, study, and reflect. The most important aspect, though, is to help you as you adjust to the role of being a widow.

Take time to ponder what you read. Don't expect an instant cure for all your problems. Work on them one at a time. Time is one of the greatest treatments used by the

Great Healer. Through this process you will become stronger as a woman. More importantly, as you work your way through the process of grieving, your faith in the Lord will deepen.

Your Sister,
Jan Sheble

"Each of you should look not only to your own interests, but also to the interests of others" (Phil. 2:4).

ONE

"He's Gone"

Whether the term used is, "He's gone . . . he's expired . . . he's passed away . . . or he's no longer here," the sting is still the same. It is over. Your husband is no longer alive—he is now dead.

Maybe you knew he was going to die, as Fran did. A year earlier she noticed a black spot on her husband's back. They immediately consulted with their family physician who tried to appear calm as he carefully made his examination and then referred them to a major teaching hospital. After evaluating all options, surgeons removed the black spot. The pathology report indicated that it was indeed malignant melanoma, but the prognosis was good. Computer-assisted scans of his body showed no sign of the disease. All was well. He was disease-free.

On subsequent hospital visits all continued to go well. The family resumed their normal routines. Then, one day, as he played catch with his six-year-old son, he noticed that his arm was a little sore but thought nothing about it. He took an over-the-counter painkiller. The next week, he noticed there was a definite swelling on that same arm. He made an appointment as quickly as he could. When the specialists saw him, they were alarmed and ordered additional scans of his body. The new scans indicated there were spots of the malignancy throughout his body.

The doctors began a series of experimental procedures as a desperate measure in hopes of restoring his health. He underwent rigorous chemotherapy. When they removed some of his white cells to irradiate them as part of an experimental treatment, Fran's young husband quipped to the medical staff, "Take good care of those cells; I may want them back." The technicians and doctors never cracked a smile. He thought to himself, *These people have no sense of humor at all.*

After he returned to his home, the family once again tried getting back to their normal life. It was difficult for them all, watching his health deteriorate. The children didn't understand why daddy couldn't play ball with them, or why he had to keep going back to the hospital, or why he was getting bald.

As he grew weaker, he and his wife realized that he wasn't going to get better, so they made plans to enjoy the time they had left together. Even to the very end, they kept hoping. One Sunday afternoon the Lord called him home; Fran was left a widow with two small children. She knew in her heart that he was going to die, but when the end came, it was so final.

Bravely, she made arrangements. His burial was private with only the immediate family present. Later on there was a memorial service at the church they attended. There she stood, trying to comfort the many others who mourned along with her. After the service she went home, where she was alone with her two young children.

After tucking the children into bed that night, she sat in the living room alone. She looked at the bookshelf. There were some photo albums of family vacations. She took one down and began to look through it. Maybe memories of their time together would make her feel better.

There were photos of their many trips to the beach. They all loved the surf, the saltwater, and playing in the sand. But in all those pictures the sun was shining down on them. She bit her lip and tried to fight back the tears as she thought of what that sun had done to all of their lives.

Another young woman, Ann, finally became pregnant with her first child. She and her husband eagerly awaited the birth of this child they'd hoped for so long. They opted not to ask the sex of the child beforehand. The nursery was ready with blue, just in case it was a boy. Ann faithfully went to her obstetrician. She and her husband talked often about what to name the baby as they wondered what the baby would look like. They discussed procedures to raise the child and where to send him to school.

Toward the end of the seventh month of pregnancy, Ann and her husband decided she should resign from her job and stay home to await the wonderful event. She missed the people she'd worked with, but then again, it was nice to be home. She had time to clean the house, cook special meals, and just put up her feet and rest. She had just leaned back in her reclining chair, one afternoon, when the phone rang. It was a frantic call from her husband's office. He had collapsed and been taken to the emergency room. Quickly, she drove to the hospital.

When she got to the hospital, he had already died—an aneurysm had taken his life. There she was, one day, waiting with excitement for the birth of their child and the next day she was a widow, waiting alone.

At the funeral home, she looked at the body of her husband. He lay there so still while inside her she could feel the kicking of the unborn child—very much alive. It all seemed so bizarre. After the funeral, she went home alone.

Janet had been diagnosed with breast cancer. She had been a surgical nurse, so she was aware of what needed to be done. She went through the necessary surgical procedures and chemotherapy. All this sapped her strength, but in her weakness, she realized that her husband lacked the skills to take care of her (and himself) and to discharge the usual household duties.

When she recovered from the intensity of the surgery and the ensuing treatments, she began to show her husband ways to cook, to keep the house, and to do the shopping. She was preparing him to be a widower since she was the one with the health problems.

It saddened him to think this way. After all, he hadn't signed up to be a surviving spouse. Dutifully, he watched and learned how to care for himself and the house after she was gone. He followed her through the grocery store and learned her techniques for wise shopping.

One Saturday morning he was out in yard, caring for the lawn and the flower garden, while she was inside doing small household tasks. Putting down the dust cloth, she thought, "What's taking him so long?" She went to the backdoor and peered through the window toward the flowerbed. There was her husband, lying face down on the lawn. She ran to him, but her nursing skills told her he was already gone—a heart attack. He had no prior history of heart problems, no indications whatsoever. But now he was gone; and she was the one left—with cancer.

Marcia had three children and was married to a man with alcohol and addiction problems. His behavior was very erratic. Convinced that he needed protection, he bought a revolver.

The more she tried talking to him about his behavior and the dangers, the more obstinate he became. They tried counseling, but he was not willing to change. They separated periodically and their attempts at reconciliation were brief and stormy.

Finally, when she could tolerate it no longer, she left with the children and found temporary housing in a motel. She hoped it would give her time to regroup and make decisions concerning the children. When her husband discovered where they were, he angrily tried to knock down the door of the motel room. She barricaded the door as best she could, but he repeatedly kept hammering it, hoping to break it in.

She could hear the threats though the door, "If you don't let me in, I'll kill myself!"

The children were terrified, cowering in fear. Her shouts of "Go away! Go away!" bounced off the walls as he continued to kick at the door. Those were her last words to him. He left the motel and drove to a secluded spot, pulled out a revolver, and killed himself.

She was alone with the children like many times before, but this time the aloneness was permanent. She was now a widow.

Do any of these stories bear a similarity to your experiences of being thrown into widowhood? Your husband's death may have come after a long illness. His death may have been sudden. No matter how prepared you thought you were, you were probably still in shock with the finality of it all. And, when that final curtain of death is drawn, the sting is still the same.

In my own case, the grim-faced emergency room doctors came to me with the shocking news, "We're sorry to tell you that he has passed away. Do you have any questions?"

I was stunned. I shook my head without saying anything. I couldn't speak. I didn't even wonder, at the time, why a perfectly healthy man could be vital one day and dead in a few hours. I thought he only had the flu; I never expected anything more. Surely, he'd be fine, but suddenly—he was dead.

My pastor was there to comfort me. He suggested I call the children immediately, and then gently reminded me that I needed to select a funeral home. I did all this without any tears. I was completely numb as grief began to settle in. Then friends drove me to my house.

At home, many of my church family gathered around the dining room table. We comforted each other as best we could in our pitiable way. One of my dear friends sat there in shock as he said, "The Lord didn't consult me on this. I could have given him names of people that he could have taken instead." He was grieving in his own way. As we all sat there, we prayed. Before they left, we sang praise songs that assured us the Lord would raise him up at the last day.

The next morning my two children, who lived out of state, arrived. Together we went to the funeral home to make arrangements. The funeral director went through all the formalities, getting my husband's social security number, his military records (so we could have a flag for the casket), information to file for social security death benefits, and obituary notices.

As we began arrangements for the funeral itself, he told us the hospital had not released Earl's body yet because it was decomposing rapidly. With a sinking feeling, it struck me. My husband was no longer a person. He was a body.

We all went back to my house. The hospital pathologist phoned to ask me some questions. I asked my daughter, who has a master's degree in genetics, to speak with him. Frankly, I couldn't handle any more right then. He told my daughter that her father had died of *Clostridium,* an anaerobic bacterium for which there is no known cure. The pathologist was trying to determine how he had contracted this infection. He insisted on an autopsy to try to determine the specific cause. It was a puzzle—it remains a mystery even today. The Lord seemed to indicate to me that he would give me the answer in due time when I could handle it.

The horrifying fact was that the infection kept growing in his body even after death. It caused extreme swelling, distortion, and gangrene. It was actually a profound blessing from the Lord that he died as quickly as he did. The funeral director said, "I can't do what I usually do," so we had the body cremated right after the autopsy.

Earl's choice had always been cremation, so at least we didn't have the problem of making that decision while under great stress. The biggest heartache was that none of the children, his clients, or friends had been able to say good-bye in the usual way. There was no casket, open or closed. There was only a tiny wooden box which held his remains.

My children and I put pictures of him all around the funeral home. We had pictures from his childhood and his adulthood. In the forefront was a picture of Jesus hugging a white robed person as he welcomes him into heaven. You've probably seen it.

There seemed to be an endless line of friends at the funeral home. I greeted them all, remembering the Bible verse: "Be strong in the Lord and in his mighty power" (Eph. 6:10).

The funeral itself was a time of celebration. I insisted that the funeral home play one of my favorite praise tapes while people were gathering. The director of music from my church sang *Enter In,* a song that had blessed Earl while he lived. The words ministered to all of us as the Lord truly gave us a "garment of praise instead of a spirit of despair" (Isa. 61:3).

After the service, there was a beautiful luncheon at my church. During that time, each lady gave me a rose. The bouquet was so lavish and overflowing that it almost covered the entire table. I'm told that all the grocery stores and florists in town were sold out of roses that day because of those dear sisters. What a glorious visual display of God's love as demonstrated by his daughters.

Following the luncheon, we had a private committal service. We went to our Christmas tree farm and hiked up the hill. There's no written service for such a time, so we made up our own. We prayed and then we spread Earl's ashes out there among the trees that he had nurtured and loved. I'm sure he would have said, "Great!"

My children gradually left for their own homes. Friends from my church came to stay with me whenever I felt I needed company. Letters, cards, and phone calls continued for weeks.

Then one day, when the last of the aluminum foil casseroles had been disposed of and the potted flower arrangements were beginning to look wilted and disheveled, reality began to sink in. I was alone in my family room eating a TV dinner. I was now a widow.

Maybe those memories of the time you heard, "He's gone," are so painful that you've buried them far away from your daily life. Maybe you felt intense relief when your husband finally died. Maybe you just don't want to talk about it. Maybe you talk about it to anyone who will listen. Maybe it was last week, last month, or last year. There are a multitude of "maybe" scenarios.

Whatever your circumstance, please reflect. Try to recall that time of intense bereavement. Think about how it was at first and how it is for you now. Remember that together we will be able to work our way through the memories of, "He's gone" and get to the business of rebuilding our lives.

TWO

Immediate Plans

"What am I going to do?"

No one can answer that question for you. You alone know the daily routines you and your husband had. Now there is only you. You alone have to make decisions and it's not easy.

When a loved one dies, the Lord blesses you with numbness. You may still feel numb today. It takes time to adjust to the new status of being single. There are so many decisions to be made that if you tried to tackle them all, you'd really be in a frenzy. You'd probably be "like a bird darting into a snare" (Prov. 7:23), dashing here and there, not really getting anywhere or accomplishing anything. So the Lord grants you numbness for a season.

This was part of Lydia's experience when she became a widow. After her children were in school and with her husband's encouragement, she'd enrolled in the university near her and become certified as an elementary school teacher. She enjoyed being in the classroom, and her students appreciated being in her class.

When her husband became ill, she had to take some days off. During the months of determining just why he had such an incessant cough, she stood by him. But when they found the coughs were due to an incurable lung condition, she had to take even more time away from her classroom.

When the end came for her husband, she found that this experience had drained her of any emotion she had. She was totally numb. Someone would ask her a question, and all she could do was stare blankly and nod her head.

Following the funeral, she said to herself, *I just can't go into the classroom tomorrow. I have nothing to give those children.*

Her colleagues tried to come to her aid. Several of the part-time teachers offered to cover her classes. Her supervisor at the school didn't agree with this plan. He felt she'd taken enough time off.

That young widow, in a state of extreme numbness, had to go back to the classroom only a week after her husband's funeral. As she sat at her desk, she didn't even have the energy to cry. She couldn't even ask herself, *What am I doing here?* She just went through all the motions of following lesson plans and grading papers. Making decisions became impossible.

Those of you who've been through it know that even the most insignificant things require decisions, but they're

hard to make when you're numb and in the process of grieving. Still you have to do something.

Perhaps you begin with those day-to-day adjustments of
your life. You may have had to change your time of getting up
or going to bed. If your husband had been an early riser, you
may find yourself getting up earlier than you used to just to
do those chores he always did—bringing in the morning
paper, starting the coffee, or adjusting the thermostat.

Mildred was an older widow whose husband had been in
a nursing home for most of the summer and the fall. By the
time he finally passed away, she'd already planned the arrangements. She felt prepared for all contingencies.

Valiantly, she went through all the motions of receiving
friends at the funeral home, the service, and the interment. Back
at her home, she would often sit looking out the window, knowing she had done all she could. As she sat there in her rocking
chair with her hands folded in her lap, she watched as the sky
became gray. Flakes of snow soon began to fall making a delicate
pattern of lace on the fallen leaves. *How pretty,* she thought. *Such
a nice way to help me concentrate on the beauty of this place where I live.*

Soon, though, the snow began to pile up in the driveway.
She rubbed her arthritic hands together trying to relieve the
pain. She sighed as she watched the snow and wondered,
Who will shovel the driveway? This may seem like a trivial decision to an onlooker, but it's just one of those unplanned for
decisions that face most widows.

There are many big and little decisions you will face:
Should you sell the house? Stay where you are? Change your
job? Or run away to Tahiti?

Barbara and her husband had been renting a small house for themselves and their only child. After her husband's funeral she very deliberately went back to that house, packed up their meager belongings, and left. She rented another little house on the other side of town thinking that getting away would surely make her life more bearable. Not so!

The standard rule for most widows is not to make any momentous decisions for at least a year. It's too tempting to run away, if not to Tahiti, then to anywhere other than staying where all the pain happened. But remember, your pain goes along with you wherever you go.

It's a little like facing a huge hill you know you need to climb. That hill is your grief. You may try to go around it, but your most efficient and long lasting solution is to start at the bottom and begin your climb. When Barbara tried to run away by moving across town, she soon found that her grief had moved right along with her.

Julia's husband had been an invalid for about a year before he died. She'd had ramps built to the doors of their home. She fixed up a downstairs bedroom for him and became his primary caregiver. Toward the end, when it was crucial, she did have to call for outside help, but was determined to keep him at home until the end.

When he finally passed away, she came back to that house which had been altered so much to facilitate his care. She chose to stay in that house, but all those modifications were constant reminders of his illness. In her mind she could still picture him limping and leaning to one side as she tugged to get his wheelchair up the ramp. She could still feel the pull on her muscles as she struggled to get him out of the wheel-chair and into the hospital bed she'd rented.

She gritted her teeth and called for workmen to remove the ramps and the other evidence of the trials they'd gone through in the past year. In her newly bereaved state, she forced herself to say: *I know I need to do this. The sooner I get it done, the sooner I'll be able to cope.*

Unless your circumstances are such that changes are imperative, it may be a wise idea to stay where you are and let your numbness carry you through this place where all that pain happened. You're not being weak; you're just going through a necessary process.

If being in the same bed where the two of you slept is diffi-cult, move to another room in the house if you can. If that's not an option, try changing the location of the bed and the other items in the room. Purchase a different set of sheets, bedspread, or quilt. Feel free to buy some overtly feminine items to help in the adjustment to your new status as a single woman.

Look in the closet where his clothes are. More decisions! What to do with them? I've known of those who shut the door on that closet, for awhile, at the time of the death. On the other hand, some widows find comfort in having his pajamas or his flannel shirt close to them.

Lillie was so distressed at the thought of seeing her hus-band's clothes hanging there limp and lifeless that she found it impossible to select the proper clothes for her husband's burial—a friend had to do it for her. She thought she would be better next week and take care of it then. She was one of those who poured bags of mothballs into the closet and shut the door.

The next week, though, did not come for a long time. It was two years before she forced herself to open that door again. Those painful wounds of sorrow were reopened. Seeing his shirt, his shoes, his cap, brought her to her knees as she cried deep tears of grief.

The best plan seems to be to clean out the closet right away. Have someone with you who can think objectively and is strong enough emotionally and physically to easily carry full plastic bags. Sometimes a widow will have the notion that perhaps a mistake was made in telling her that her husband had died. She imagines that he'll discover she's gotten rid of his things and be mad at her. This may sound unrealistic to some, but those who've gone through the path of grief, can probably understand Lillie's concern.

If you have put off the task of cleaning out his clothes, do it now. You're not being disloyal to him. You're just doing what you have to do to get on with the task the Lord has assigned you. And that task is living.

What do you do with his other things? His golf clubs? His power tools? The sooner you find homes for these items, the better off you'll be. As long as they're around, those things will continue to haunt you and remind you of what once was but now is gone. Think of the blessings your donations can be. Perhaps a beginning golfer would be grateful for your generous gift. It's not that you're glad your husband died, it's just one way of looking for positives.

And speaking of looking, check your left hand. Do you still wear your wedding ring? To wear it or not can be a tough choice. It's a totally personal one. To some it's a comfort. To others it's a painful reminder of what has happened.

Of course, some widows choose to put their wedding rings on their right hand. Others have put their husband's wedding ring on a chain to wear around the neck as a remembrance. At her husband's funeral, Zoë chose to wear his wedding band on her thumb. All during the service she twisted it round and round, feeling the smoothness of the metal as she thought about the time when she'd placed it on her husband's finger. Sometimes wedding rings can be a sweet remembrance. Other times they can be difficult reminders.

Look around your house. Are there other reminders that bother you? Maybe there's a picture on the wall that you and he chose when you went away for your anniversary, and looking at that picture brings back tearful memories. Should you take it down and store it in an out-of-the-way place for now? It might be a good idea for a few months. The reason I suggest you do this is because the picture could be a blessing-in-disguise, later on, when you're stronger. You *will* be stronger you know, in time, with the Lord's help.

Day-to-day living is not easy. Sort out what's necessary and cope as best you can. The world may be watching you to see how you're adjusting to your new status as a widow, especially if you're a Christian.

Although I know it was the strength and the shield of the Lord carrying me through my entire trauma, I still tried to be strong for everyone else. The night my husband died, one of our teenage friends admired the rainbow shoestrings I had in my sneakers. Without a word, I went to my closet where I had a supply of them and brought her a pair. "Wow! What strength!" everyone said. A few weeks later, another dear friend needed to talk over her problems. She came to my house and we sat in my family room and cried together over her problem.

Strength! I was so strong in my living, in my adjustment, and in most areas. But then I would find myself in the bathroom throwing up. You see, my body just couldn't take the tension I was imposing on it. My body wanted to stay numb for a season, and I was pushing it to the limit, trying to be strong.

Just a word of caution: be strong, but allow yourself to be weak at the same time. Let others help you through these difficult first days. When I hesitated to accept help, a very wise Christian friend reminded me that I was robbing her of a blessing by not letting her serve me. That was a very powerful message to me since I viewed myself as the *strong* one!

Whether you're weak or strong, you still have to deal with decisions and annoyances. You get an information form to complete at the dentist's office and you have to check "single." Do you feel single? On your car insurance, you're single. Your tax forms . . . Single! Single! Single! Single!

In other words, you're alone. But the Lord reminds you, you're not alone: "Never will I leave you; never will I forsake you" (Heb. 13:5).

Even though the world with its information forms calls us *single*, we're not alone. Our Lord, the true husband of us all, is with us. So, we wash away the tears, sit up straight, write the rest of the thank-you notes, look at the sympathy cards one more time, and then get on with the adjustment to the new life that God has called us to.

THREE

The First Year

Everyone says that the first year of anything is the hardest. This is certainly true with adjusting to being widowed. There's the first Christmas without him, the first Valentine's Day, the first wedding anniversary, the first . . .

Once the immediate shock has worn off, you figure you should have it all together. You've made all the arrangements. You've made some decisions concerning your life and your future. But then you find the tears flowing and you shake a figurative fist at the Lord and ask, "Why?" One minute you're a together person, the next you're an angry toddler.

Lisa's husband died suddenly. She never had a chance to say goodbye. He was there one minute and gone the next. In her thinking, the most ironic part of all this was that he always took care of himself. He didn't drink. He never smoked. He exercised daily and kept his weight in check. It reminded her of the bumper sticker that said: EAT RIGHT. EXERCISE. AND DIE ANYWAY. She asked the Lord, "Why?"

She thought becoming more active in her inner city church would help her feel better. She volunteered at the soup kitchen each Wednesday. On the first day she was scheduled to work, she drove into the church parking lot and saw a man lying on the back steps of the church. He had drawn himself into a fetal position. His beard was unkempt, his clothes were filthy, and he reeked of alcohol. She parked her car as far away from the drunk as she could. She got out of her car, jammed her thumb down on the button to engage the automatic locks, and muttered, *God, why in the world would you let this man live and allow my husband to die?*

She took several deep breaths and tried to compose herself before going into the church to do the volunteer work she had promised she would do. But that day she approached the volunteer task with little enthusiasm as she thought about her life, her loss, and the man who was still living. She began to think, *What is the matter with me?*

You, too, may wonder, *What's the matter with me? Am I going crazy?*

Don't worry; you're not going crazy. We all go through those feelings during the first year; some even longer. It's part of adjusting and reorienting to a new situation. So, if you feel hot or cold . . . on again, off again . . . up and down, you're not

alone. It's like a yo-yo. Your feelings will go up and down . . .
up and down. You can't help it. The Lord gave you those
emotions. He understands when you vacillate. And part of
that yo-yo experience makes you feel numb one moment
and experience intense emotions the next.

Ida's husband had suffered a number of debilitating
strokes. She tried to take care of him in their home, but the
sheer physical work became too much for her. Reluctantly,
she searched for a nursing home for him.

The closest and best one she could find was three hours
from their home. She made that trip day after day, and kept
thinking that he'd get better soon. But the days melted one
into another; days became weeks, and weeks became months.
When she saw his health continue to deteriorate, she realized
she had to do something about the logistics of her lifestyle.

She opted to sell her home and relocate closer to the
nursing home. Her home sold within two months. She
moved to an apartment in the city where the nursing home
was. Her daily trips were shorter, so it made that part of her
life easier. Every day she would back her car out of her designated parking spot and go to the nursing home. The medical staff there all knew her. Their cheery hellos helped her
focus less on what she knew she'd see once she reached her
husband's bedside.

She would sit there, holding his hand, knowing that even
if he appeared unresponsive, it was important to keep on talking to him and maintain an upbeat conversation. So she told
him stories about the children and the grandchildren. She
talked to him about the weather, and the vacations they had

taken. She left his bedside only to visit the restroom or to make a quick trip to the vending machines where she had a semblance of a meal.

Those daily trips went on and on for another nineteen months. When he finally passed away and she'd taken care of all the arrangements, she was exhausted from the strain of what she had been through.

She'd wake up each morning and think, *I must get ready to go to the nursing home.* Then she would remember what happened. *What will I do with myself today?*

She saw how hard it was to change from being on that treadmill of daily visits. Because she had concentrated on the care of her husband for so long, she didn't really have friends in the area. Now she had to decide if she should stay there or move. She found it very difficult to decide what to eat for lunch each day, much less make decisions regarding larger issues like moving.

Widows frequently find that concentration is almost impossible. At the time of my husband's death, I was enrolled in a correspondence course in biblical eschatology. That project had to be put on hold for a long time. As a matter of fact, I still haven't gotten back to it.

I also found that I couldn't even watch television. Those shows that graphically show emergency rooms were too painful for me to watch. Documentaries or news stories about strange illnesses were impossible to handle. I couldn't read a book, a magazine, or a newspaper. I couldn't even read the Bible! But I knew my heavenly Father understood. He saw me through even that. I know within my wounded heart that his love directed my heart when I felt like giving up.

During that first year, you may feel very fragile and unable to cope with even the smallest things. One day I was asked to take care of a small baby, but I simply could not do it. Even though it caused some misunderstanding, I had to say, "No, I can't tackle that task."

If it's any consolation, months later I was able to baby-sit for not one, but several children for a number of days. Be patient, my widowed sister. Strength is coming in the morning of our grieving: "Weeping may remain for a night, but rejoicing comes in the morning" (Ps. 30:5).

Speaking of mornings, you may find you either can't sleep or have to force yourself to get up in the morning. Claudine was a widow who hid away in her family room. She dozed most of the days in a lounge chair. She ate there, she slept on the sofa there, and she watched television alone there. When she had to go out to the store for groceries, she went late at night so she wouldn't see anyone she knew.

Her purchases weren't always the wisest for her health. She bought snack food, sodas, chocolate candy, or anything that appealed to her at the time. For the entire first year of her bereavement, she hid in the comfort zone of her family room. When she emerged from her cocoon, she had gained forty pounds. When her acquaintances asked what happened, she felt even worse and retreated again to her family room, drawing the drapes and reaching for another box of candy.

Other widows are even more frenzied. Sleep is hard to come by. Some widows lay awake at nights and worry about the noises they hear or the bills that they have to pay.

Are all the doors locked?

What's that strange squeaking noise?

Did I remember to mail that government form?

Some who can't sleep seem to have a compulsion to keep going. There's so much to do. Once there were two to take care of the house, the yard, and the car. Now there's only you to do it all. It can give rise to sleepless nights. As the psalmist says: "Troubles without number surround me" (Ps. 40:12).

Dianna was a young widow with two children. She had lots of sleepless nights. Her husband had known he was going to die, so they had talked about what she would do when he was gone. Her parents had invited her to move back to her hometown to live with them. Her husband and she agreed that it was a good idea but . . . how and when? While she was in the throes of watching her husband in his illness, she'd put the thought of returning home in the back of her mind.

One day the inevitable happened—her husband was gone. She was alone. Her children were without their father. She thought about the plan to return to her hometown. It would mean leaving all her friends. Her children would have to change schools and make new friends. Could she face returning to where she had grown up? Could she be there in the town where she and her husband had met, fallen in love, and married? A myriad of thoughts kept rolling around in her mind, day and night—but especially at night. She felt very alone and incomplete as she spent many sleepless hours. You may feel very

incomplete now that there's only you to take care of the
_____ (insert any answer of your choice).

There's a psychological concept known as *gestalt*. This premise centers on the fact that humans function best when there is closure, when things are all together with no loose ends. When we lose a husband, we've also lost our completeness. There are loose ends. Things are not all together, and we feel very incomplete. It's not that we can't rebuild our lives to make them complete again. It's just that it takes time and lots of adjustment for us to arrive at the point of being as together a person as we can be.

During that first year, you might find yourself doing what you feel are bizarre things. You see something new and think: *I must tell him about this. He'll be very interested in how they . . .* and then you remember!

You see a man who walks like him, who has hair the same color as his, or who is wearing a shirt like one of his. Your heart skips a beat as you raise your hand to wave to him, and then you remember.

How bizarre, you say to yourself.

You may even be angry with yourself for being so stupid. Remember, you're not going crazy. Your thoughts are not bizarre. You're just working out your adjustment to what has happened.

The reminders of what once were can come crashing in on you especially hard during that first year. You may still get phone calls for him. My husband was a self-employed forester consultant with his office in our home. Some of his clients didn't know he had died. They would call and ask me in rather severe tones why he'd missed an appointment. I had to answer those calls and tell the story over and over again. Those were painful times, but I understand now it was a necessary step I had to take.

Using the checkbook is another reminder of what was. Our personal checking account had both names imprinted on the checks. There they were right in front of me every time I had to write a check for the utilities, the credit cards, everything. At first I put a line through his name on the checks. When I found that to be too depressing, I simply ordered new checks with only my name on them.

The mail addressed to him was another reminder. Sometimes you have to write back to whomever and explain (once again) what happened. It may or may not be a comfort to know that several years later, you still may get mail addressed to Mr. and Mrs._____.

Among the mail addressed only to him may be those cheery notices: YOU HAVE BEEN APPROVED FOR A CREDIT CARD. Personally, I find it hard to believe that they would even suggest they had done a thorough search to determine his eligibility.

And then there's the mail that's my favorite when I need a laugh. It's been years since my husband died and I've relocated several times since then. Yet, mail addressed only to Mr. Sheble finds its way to me. When that mail offers him a great deal on health insurance, I almost have to giggle and think, *A lot of good that will do him now.*

And then I remind myself that he's in a perfect place where there's no need for health insurance.

Although there will be reminders all around you of him and what once was, there will also be times when you begin to emerge from that cocoon of grief. You may feel moments of joy when the Lord speaks to you. But even a twinge of joy may make you feel guilty. How can I be happy when my husband is dead? Doesn't everyone know I can't forget him? It's during those times that we need to look at what the apostle Paul wrote: "Forgetting what is behind and straining toward what is ahead" (Phil. 3:13).

Forgetting doesn't mean erasing it totally from your mind. You can't do that. Your life with your husband and your marriage are all part of what made you who you are. But instead of focusing on what was, you need to focus on what will be.

And before you know it, it's been a year since he died.

FOUR

Regrets

The instructor demonstrated to the class how we frequently focus on the negative. Students were asked to look at a sheet of white paper with a black dot a half-inch in diameter in the center of it. Then the instructor asked the class to tell him what they saw. The majority said it was the black dot. They totally ignored the pure white sheet of paper and concentrated only on the black dot. The purpose of this exercise was to show that most of us look at the negative, not the positive. And when we look back on our experiences with regrets, aren't we focusing on that black dot?

After Earl died, someone asked me if I had any regrets. I commented that my only regret was that

I didn't beg him to come out to California with me. I went there to help my daughter following the birth of her second child, while he remained home alone on the East Coast. I was there for a month. All the while a voucher for a free flight to anywhere sat on his desk. The bottom line was that four months later, he was dead and he never saw his grandchild. My regret was that I didn't make him come to Southern California when his granddaughter was born.

Marti had talked for years about how she was going to leave her husband. She felt that he was too busy to notice her; she wanted more out of life. He had his own interests that didn't include her. Because he was an avid golfer, much of his free time was spent playing golf at their country club. When he was home, he read his golf magazines incessantly. She would sit seething in her easy chair because he seemed to pay more attention to his friends and his hobby than to her.

She decided she would counter this by seeking her own interests. She always enjoyed books so she volunteered to work in the church library. She delighted in stocking the shelves with the books as they were returned, but noticed as she placed them back on the shelves that they hadn't been properly catalogued. She took on the challenge of doing the necessary cataloguing and found it to be extremely rewarding. Frequently, she would work on repairing damaged books that had been abused. She learned the skill of covering books in plastic library bindings. She spent every day in that library. She created displays to promote new books as they arrived. Sometimes she would focus on seasonal topics in these displays trying to make them as attractive as she could.

The church members noticed how much the appearance of the library had improved. They appreciated being able to locate books using her system. It was then that she finally felt she was, indeed, a worthwhile person.

In the evenings she had to go home and face her everyday existence. She made mental plans on how she'd move out. She would tell him that one of these days he'd be sorry. She licked her imaginary wounds and waited for the opportune time to tell him.

But that opportune time never came. He was driving home one day when a drunk driver hit him head-on. In an instant he was gone. Her anger with him for presumed rejections melted into her regrets. She still went to the church library daily. She found herself spending time in the section on grief and recovery. She was searching for solace among the shelves of books.

One evening, as she was crossing the church parking lot to her car, to drive home a summer storm arose. She looked up at the gray clouds as they started gathering and colliding into one another. The turmoil in the skies reminded her of how she perceived life with her husband. But then, as she continued to look up, she thought of how peaceful the sky was just beyond those clouds. It was in that peaceful setting where she now knew her husband sojourned. She swallowed hard as she whispered with only a little regret, "Enjoy your *forever* golf game."

For me, as time has flown by since Earl's death, I've thought a lot about the "what ifs" I still face. Traces of them still hang around to haunt me. I regret that I seldom told Earl how much I appreciated him.

I never have been the best of housekeepers. Over the years, I stayed very busy with working and volunteering. Friends would ask how I managed to get so much done in such a short time. I'd answer them, "I don't do housework!" My husband would laugh and say, "That's true, she doesn't!" Although it seemed all right with him, I wondered sometimes if I had let him down. But it's too late now, and I have to get on with the business of living.

Now that he's gone, I'd never imply that I have my role as a widow all together. In talking with other widows, I've found that many of us deal with regrets, often directly related to the actual death of our husband. For example, we may say things such as:

"Why didn't I recognize the signs of his heart attack?"

"If only he hadn't driven down that road at that particular time."

"I should have known he was sick."

"What if he'd gone to the doctor months before it was too late?"

"Why didn't he give up smoking?"

In most of these statements, we're demonstrating our guilt. We're focusing once again on that black dot instead of the pure white paper. Notice, too, the operative words in these comments and questions.

"Why?"

"If only."

"I should have."

"What if?"

These are questions we think we're asking ourselves, but we're really asking the Lord why he chose to take our husbands at that particular time. By asking these questions indicates we forget what the Scriptures tell us about our time here on earth: "There is a time for everything, and a season for every activity under heaven: a time to be born and a time to die" (Eccl. 3:1, 2).

In our frail human way we ask the Almighty Lord of the Universe *why* and *what if,* yet he remains on his throne waiting for us to understand and come to terms with what he has allowed to happen for his ultimate purposes. Death was never part of God's plan. Death is directly related to sin in the world. And until that blessed time comes when we enter eternal Glory, death will be part of our lot on this planet.

Cathy was a widow who truly had regrets. As she sat in her chair looking out the window, she remembered how her life had been the last few years while her husband was alive. For many years, her marriage had been rather humdrum. There was no specific reason she could pinpoint as to why it was. It had just happened. Her husband was faithful to her, was always a good provider, and though his communication skills were not sparkling, he was a good man.

Through the years, there were many times when she felt ignored. To her, the monotony of the marriage was most evident after the children were grown and on their own. She'd sit in the spare bedroom reading romance novels. As she read and pictured in her mind the ways those fictional couples lived, she would sigh and mutter, *My life is never like that.*

She began to watch television soap operas and found herself lost in a world she could only dream about. Those men seemed so romantic. The women were so pampered. These men would take their wives to the finest restaurants where they served entrees such as pheasant under glass. She'd sigh again as she thought of the times that her husband suggested they go out to eat. His choice invariably would be a modest restaurant. They'd sit there mutely, never having a conversation that meant anything. What had happened to them?

Her husband would sometimes tell her he really loved her, but she couldn't even respond. Generally she'd smile weakly and change the subject. Occasionally he'd suggest intimacy. Again she would smile weakly, get up out of bed, and go to the living room where she'd turn on the television to watch late night movies. He would lie alone in the darkness of their bedroom; shaking his head as he wondered what had happened to the girl he married.

Then one day he was gone. It was then that she realized their time together had been tainted by her unrealistic expectations. She kept reminding herself that he was a good man. He did cherish her in his own way. She wished she had cherished him. She wished she hadn't spurned him as he suggested sexual relations, but now it was too late. She threw out the romance novels; and she made an effort to change her television preferences.

The good that came out of this was that she began to cherish and soak in all the experiences in her life. The sky seemed bluer to her. The aroma of blossoming flowers seemed more intense. She began to realize how much her God cherished her. With his perfect grace, it made no difference to the Lord that she'd been such an ungrateful person—not appreciating her husband, their marriage, and their relationship. God not only wiped away her tears of grief but also her tears of regret.

One day, a friend of hers began to complain about her husband. Cathy reprimanded her in a stern but pleasant voice. "Cherish him," she said. Later this friend would frequently remind her how much that one little comment had meant to her in her own marriage.

A lot of the regrets we face as widows center around our marriages or our relationship with our husbands. We all have feet of clay. We all make mistakes because we're human. Even the apostle Paul struggled with mistakes: "I do not understand what I do. For what I want to do I do not do, but what I hate I do—it is sin living in me" (Rom. 7:15-17).

We probably will never understand why we did what we did, but now it's too late to set things right or apologize. Maybe you had the habit of overspending. And he, like most husbands, probably complained about it. Then you would fight. As you look back, you may be saying to yourself, *I shouldn't have argued with him.*

Maybe he always wanted to vacation on the beach, but you insisted on going to the mountains. Dutifully, he would go along with what you wanted. Have you since said to yourself, *Why was I so bullheaded?*

Maybe you considered divorce. Maybe you even separated for a time. Maybe you berated him, humiliated him, or said spiteful things. Maybe you participated in that popular practice of male bashing. Maybe you were vocal in your anger at him, seethed underneath, became resentful, or unresponsive to him. Today you may look back on those times and say, *If only I'd been more of an understanding wife.*

Look back over these past few paragraphs and notice the:

What if?

Why?

Should have.

In these scenarios, you may say you're not blaming the Lord; you're blaming yourself for your human shortcomings. But wait a minute! Who made you? God, your Creator did. He knows your human frailties. He knows you grieve for those things you've done and for those things you've not done, but he still loves you. He knows your deep regrets. It does no good to beat yourself up over the past. The Lord understands why you said those things that caused deep hurt. He knows how your husbands may have said things that cut you deeply, too. He understands completely and is waiting to comfort you for whatever has happened in your marriages or in your life.

There are other "what ifs" and you could conjecture for years about "what if," but would it get you anywhere? Maybe it would give you some ideas for romance novels, but it probably wouldn't help move you down the path the Lord has chosen for you. "It is not for man to direct his steps" (Jer. 10:23).

So, rather than dwelling on the "what ifs" and the "if onlys," your task as daughters of the God of Creation is to look up to him and know that he will direct your way. He has allowed circumstances to touch you, but he's in ultimate control and knows what is best for you. Rest in this: "I am the LORD, your God, who teaches you what is best for you, who directs you in the way you should go" (Isa. 48:17).

FIVE

Single Parenting

R honda was a young widow with three children, ages four, six, and nine. Her husband had collapsed one day in the living room of their house. The children looked on in wide-eyed astonishment as she attempted to perform CPR, but in her heart she knew he was gone. When the ambulance arrived, the medical personnel confirmed that, indeed, it was too late. The children watched as the ambulance took their father away. They looked up at their mother and wondered why her face looked the way it did.

During the time surrounding the funeral, various friends and relatives cared for the children. This lasted for a time, but then the offers of help ceased and she was alone with her children. She'd been a homeschooling parent, so at least that helped to keep her mind off what had happened. But she noticed that one by one the children's behavior started slipping. When she asked them to obey, they wouldn't. The youngest one reverted to wetting his bed. When they went shopping, she couldn't keep them under control. When they whined for candy and cookies, it was just too much trouble to say, "No."

Evenings, after she finally got the children to bed, was the only time she had to herself. In a sense she was grateful for the quiet, even though it was painfully evident that she was very alone. Nights seemed endless. And in the mornings when the children arose, the pattern of homeschooling and discipline began all over again.

She had always thought her husband would be there. She considered him to be much more than just a husband. He was her confidant, her lover, her support, and her best friend. And now she had to go on without him. One morning her nine-year-old asked in a defiant voice, "Why couldn't you make Daddy live?" It was then that the tears she had stifled began to flow. She couldn't even answer that question because there was no answer for it.

I always referred to my husband as my best friend, but with that best friend gone the world can be a difficult place in which to live. With your best friend no longer alive, who else in the world cares about you or your kids? I'm sure you've guessed the answer to that. The one who cares about you, your kids, and your situation is our heavenly Father. He's eager to be your best friend, your advisor, your confidant.

In our Christian vernacular we sometimes dress up worry and call it "concern," but the practice remains the same. We are letting the details get in the way of our thinking. One way to address your worries or concerns is to make lists. Write down what's bothering you right now, this child or that one, future college bills, the lack of a father figure, or whatever's on your mind. Put the list aside for a few days. Then go back to it. Add and delete items. When you feel it's fairly complete, cross off the items that are out of your control for now. Later, you may be able to address these issues but, for now, put them on hold because, "Each day has enough trouble of its own" (Matt. 6:34).

Prioritize the remaining items. First, you will do this. Second, you will do that . . . and so on. There can be a genuine feeling of release when you don't try to solve all your problems at once. It can be compared with the question: "How do you eat a whole elephant?" The answer: "One spoonful at a time." In your new single-parent status, you'll find it easier to go on day to day when you have specific, attainable goals to work toward, one spoonful at a time.

Another benefit of breaking down mammoth problems into little ones is that just making this plan will help you overcome the fears you find creeping up on you. It can help you separate unrealistic fears from those that can be real threats. Sometimes, fear gives you a clue that you are being realistic about your situation and are facing issues you need to deal with right now.

As an example, you and your husband may have had reciprocal wills. What happens now? Instead of being afraid, see your attorney and have your will revised to reflect your current situation. You may need to look for ways to assure that should anything happen to you, persons of your choice would care for your children. In time you may have to revise your will as your children grow or other circumstances occur. Do the same thing with your life insurance. The situation has changed. It's time to look details over and make concrete plans for what you need to do to protect your children.

Just as worrying is unproductive, so fear can be unproductive as well. But when you deal with a personal will, insurance, and other legal matters, don't fret about it. Instead, face it head on. By using this direct approach, you will assure yourself you're making progress. And remember, dear sister, that fear, fretting, and worry are indications that you need to place your trust in your heavenly Father who cares for you and your children.

Edie's children were all adults, except for her severely retarded son, who was confined to a wheelchair. Her husband had always tried to include this son in his fishing trips, jaunts to the grocery store, errands, or just for walks.

As he went on these trips, errands, and walks, the other children felt they were not as important to their dad as their handicapped brother was. At times the other children would ask their dad if he would take them to a ballgame. His usual response was that the local stadium was not handicap accessible, so he couldn't take them.

As they grew up, the other children eventually left home. Several of them moved to other states. One day, the mother looked around at the empty house and thought about her life. Even though it seemed they were *empty nesters,* they really weren't. And then one day, her husband had a fatal heat attack. The disabled son couldn't understand what had happened. He kept looking around the house for his dad. When Edie could stand it no longer, she decided to sell the house. She thought the change in location would help her son realize that his daddy was no longer there, but it didn't. He still wheeled his chair around the new house, looking for the person who was not there and never would be again.

Jeannette had only one son. From the time he was very little, people would remark how much he resembled his daddy. He had the same blue eyes and his blonde hair curled just a little. When he was trying to solve a puzzling situation, he'd furrow his brow, just like his daddy. One fateful day the physician told Jeannette's husband that he had a debilitating disease. Nothing could be done to stop the progression of his disease or prolong the inevitable.

After her husband's death, she focused even more on how her son was so like his father. She could almost see her husband in the way the boy walked. And, as he grew, he resembled him more and more. Even when his voice changed, it was a lot like that of her late husband's. As long as she had him with her, she could remember her husband and be comforted. When the time came for him to go away to college, she found herself grieving all over again.

You may be thinking about the fact that you're the only parent your children have. If this is true, you'll be well advised to take care of yourself. Get a medical checkup and follow your doctor's advice. If your single parenting situation is preying on your mind incessantly, get some help in the form of professional counseling. Many churches offer it free or at very low cost.

Some days you may feel that it's just too much trouble to take care of yourself. You may be tempted to let yourself go, but you need to remind yourself that you'll be at your best as a parent when you feel good about yourself, your appearance, and your worth as a person. It's vital to remind yourself that you *are* a daughter of the heavenly King. There can be no better esteem than that. So lift up your head, praise the Lord, and rejoice in your own special way that he is your Lord. He doesn't want you to rely only on yourself; he wants you to totally rely on him. He tells you, "Cast your cares on the LORD and he will sustain you; he will never let the righteous fall" (Ps. 55:22).

As a single mom, you need to reach out to find those who can understand, who've been where you are, or who are there now. He will provide others with whom you can interact. Where do you find them? Sometimes churches have groups for single parents. The Parent/Teacher organization at your children's school may be a source of potential friends who can identify with you and understand your situation.

There is also information on the internet about single parent organizations. Many of these single-parenting groups have chapters across the country. They offer educational, family, and adult social/recreational activities. They stress that they don't exist for the purpose of dating, but to serve families where there is only one parent.

You also need additional social contacts so that you can have other adults to interact with. When my children were preschoolers, my husband traveled four days each week. I found myself looking for anyone, even a neighborhood child, over the age of six.

Talk to me! I need some conversation that's above the level of nursery rhymes.

Perhaps you feel the same way. Seek and find other adults to talk with. Don't expect to find fast and true friendships in an instant. Go cautiously but consistently.

You may want to change your location. Perhaps moving to another town would help. Perhaps moving back to where you grew up would lead you to those friends who were previously part of your life.

Mary had two young children. She opted to move back into her parents' home where she had grown up. It was a large home with an inviting yard shaded by oak trees. Her marriage had been a very happy one and she found that now, without her husband, she yearned to be once again in safe and comfortable surroundings. So she sold her home and moved several states away. At least her son would have the advantage of a father figure in his grandfather.

Whether you choose to relocate or stay where you are, you need to think of your children. They are going through a grief period just as you are, so watch for signs of stress in them. They'll give you clues about where they are as they work through the problem of not having a father anymore.

When I was teaching preschool, I had a child in my class who had just lost his father to a heart attack. This young lad didn't verbalize his feelings, but as I watched him play I noticed that every day he would go to the housekeeping corner. He'd be sure to take with him life-size puppets of the three bears—papa bear, mama bear, and baby bear. Every day, all three puppets had to be there with him. This went on for several weeks. Then one day I noticed he only took the mama bear and the baby bear. He was working out his adjustment in his own way, on his own terms.

In the same way, your children probably are giving you clues about where they are in their adjustment. Be as gentle with them as you can be. When they ask questions, be honest with them. Their father didn't go away or leave them—he died. It wasn't because they misbehaved. It wasn't because God was mad at them. It was just God's perfect timing. You need to have faith in the fact that children can be gently led into trusting God's ways.

If you are feeling by now that this is all overwhelming, close your eyes and say to yourself: "Those who hope in the LORD will renew their strength. They will soar on wings like eagles; they will run and not grow weary, they will walk and not be faint" (Isa. 40:31).

SIX

Loneliness

S ally was experiencing loneliness following the death of her husband. She breathed a deep sigh as she told her son how lonely she was. The reply was not one she expected.

"That's the way it's supposed to be. You have to expect it to be that way."

It stung beyond belief.

Loneliness happens to widows at differing times. You can be in a crowd but you're not really part of that crowd. Think of how restaurants are usually set up. There are tables for two or four, but rarely for three or five. Suppose, in your newly widowed state, you go to a restaurant with two couples, friends of yours. For years, you and your husband had been going places with these same two couples. But on this occasion, the evening meal turns into a major production. You wait as the restaurant's staff attempt to create a fifth place for you, for the extra one. Your friends don't mind all the commotion of trying to seat you, but you do. It's another of those painful reminders of what was and is no more.

Paula was an attractive widow who was eager to rejoin her married friends. Before the death of her husband, the couples would frequently go out together to the movies. Sometimes they would get together at one of their homes to play cards or board games. Now, whenever she tried to get together with these friends, there were various excuses as to why they couldn't get together. She wondered if the other wives considered her a threat, now that she was unattached. Certainly she had no plans to break up any marriages. It was almost as if these couples (and the wives in particular) were afraid that if they associated with her they might catch the "leprosy" of being widowed—the leprosy of facing their own mortality.

Recently I heard the story of a widow who finally got up the courage to attend a sit-down dinner at a church. Shyly, she entered the building, following the aroma of the turkey dinner to the gymnasium. She slipped into a chair at one of the closest tables and looked around her. Each table was set with fresh flowers and there were eight chairs.

As more people arrived they began to fill in the chairs at her table and soon only one chair was vacant. A waiter came to her and said, "There's a couple here who need to sit together. Surely you won't mind moving." She nodded feebly and moved to another table but the same thing happened again ... and then again. Finally, she started toward the door just to get away. However, one couple noticed what had happened and they insisted that the waiters add a ninth place to their table for her. Can you imagine her feelings?

Nancy worked as an historical interpreter in a touristy, restored village. She truly enjoyed her work. There was always so much to learn about these settlers and the community in which they had settled. She eagerly told visitors about the history of the community. Frequently, part of the interpretation was demonstrating a craft or a skill from the eighteenth and nineteenth centuries.

As a means of sharing the history, costumes were replicated in the appearance of eighteenth-century dress. The ladies, in the style of that day, wore different colored ribbons as ties on their white head covering. The same colored ribbons were also used to lace up their very best dress. The colors of these ribbons designated various peer groups within the community. The cherry-colored ribbons were for children and the pink ones for unmarried ladies. While she was married, she wore light blue ribbons.

When her husband died, she took a few weeks off, but then she kept telling herself that she could dispel her loneliness if she went back to work. A few days before she was scheduled to return to work, she went into the costume department at the restoration village. There she was given white ribbons to indicate that she was now single—a widow to be more precise.

It was difficult to face the questions of the visitors to the tourist village. When she heard the question, "Why do you wear white ribbons, while the lady greeter at the front door wears blue ones?" She had to explain the significance of the different colored ribbons. As she did, her loneliness became more pronounced. She was the widowed one.

One day, as she was walking to her lunch break, a visitor stopped her on the street and asked the infamous question. She explained yet again that the white color signified widowhood. Presuming this was only a role she was playing, the visitor quipped, "Sorry about your husband." She tried to fake a smile as she scurried toward the small breakroom where she sat alone, stifling back the tears as she tried to eat the lunch she had packed that morning.

Still, she kept working because the days were busy and generally filled with pleasant times. When school groups came for tours they were even busier. She felt as if she was helping the visitors learn more about that specific historical village.

Those times at work took care of the days. But then she had to go home and face the emptiness of her quiet house. When she got there, she'd begin her routine of trying to stay busy so she didn't have to think about how alone she was. She would change out of her costume and put on jeans and a T-shirt. There was always laundry to do since she had the responsibility of caring for her own costumes. They were linen, so of course there was starching and ironing to do to keep them looking fresh. But when she'd finished all this, she looked around the house, and it was still quiet and lonely.

I know you can relate to Nancy and the loneliness of an empty house.

Gwen heard the tick-tock of the grandfather's clock in the hall the minute she walked into her house. In the past, she would have welcomed that sound as she came into the house. It reminded her that the clock was an heirloom from her husband's family. Now, the mechanical sound echoed like a roar whenever she entered the empty house.

One day as she listened to a teaching on a Christian radio station, she heard the suggestion to keep a radio turned on to Christian music at all times in the house—day and night. She decided she'd do just that. In fact she turned a radio on in every room of her house just to keep her mind on the positives in life, rather than letting the negativism of loneliness get the best of her. Hearing the praise songs and listening to the teachings helped her fill her mind with thoughts that dissipated some of the loneliness.

Even travel can present challenges to the newly widowed. Some of the best airline deals are for you and a companion. Hotels charge just as much for one person as they do for two. On tours, cruises in particular, there's often a surcharge for singles. Traveling alone can be very lonely and costly.

Maybe you've thought about getting involved with a group for singles. Many churches have such organizations. You decide to attend a meeting, but discover that 99 percent of those who attend are single because of divorce. In most single's groups I've been in, I was asked right away, "And how long have you been divorced?"

Often these divorced people are newly single. They still bear the bruises of what they've been through. They need the tender loving care that a singles group can offer. However it's been my experience that although a divorced person and a widowed one may have similar feelings, I find I'm unable to minister to a divorced person. Nor can that divorced person truly understand where I am in my adjustment to the singles scene.

One would think and hope that Christian bookstores would have information on widowhood. Wrong! Search the shelves and you will find that books for singles pertain mostly to the divorced or to those who've never married and are still seeking for the perfect mate.

So you say to yourself, *It's true. No one cares.* You remind yourself of these words from the Bible: "I am lonely and afflicted. The troubles of my heart have multiplied" (Ps. 25:16, 17).

There must be a remedy. Maybe a conference for singles will cover the topic of widowhood. Wrong again! The widowed are usually forgotten in that arena also. I've been to some of these conferences and I know. The speakers wax eloquently on divorce and how to overcome its aftermath, but never touch the issue of being alone because of the death of a husband. Is there a solution for loneliness? Or are we to go on and on like this until we, too, are called home to be with the Lord? Are we relegated to sitting at home, eating that TV dinner, and watching the nightly news alone?

I've asked myself those same questions many times. There are no easy answers. I do know that the Lord doesn't want us to sit around wasting time until he calls us home to be with him. We are creatures who need other humans like us to interact with, to talk with, and to learn from.

Some widows choose to move into a retirement home near where their grown children live. Peg decided to do so and moved near her daughter and family. She found friends her own age to interact with, and was also able to visit her daughter's home in the evenings or on weekends. Frequently, though, she discovered they had their own friends and plans for weekends. At times, they would invite her along on their vacations, but their choice of where they wanted to go was not the same as hers. Still, she went along and tried to have the best time possible.

She also had a son living in another state. He and his family would travel every year to a seashore resort where she and her husband used to take their children for vacations. She loved that place. She had wonderful memories of the salt air, the relaxed surroundings, and the little town itself. When her son's wife phoned each year to tell her when they would be away at this resort, she'd bite her tongue and swallow hard. In her loneliness she yearned to be included and to be part of their lives.

One Sunday her pastor gave a sermon on the theme of being thankful in all things. The text was, "Give thanks in all circumstances, for this is God's will for you in Christ Jesus" (1 Thess. 5:18). At first she crossed her arms as if to brace herself. Surely this message was not meant for her. But as the teaching went on, she began to get the message of being grateful no matter what the circumstances. She realized she could be a lot worse off than she was. From that day on, she resolved to think more positively and enjoy the family and friends she did have. When traces of loneliness or neglect arose, she thought about that sermon and repeated to herself, *Give thanks in all circumstances.*

Because I've have always enjoyed learning, I tried to overcome my loneliness by going to some classes specifically designed for senior citizens. You can find these types of classes all over the world.

After one week in class, listening to the professors and interacting with the other students I realized how much I needed just to talk with others on my own level. I truly enjoy talking with people in my own age bracket. They, too, came to the classes hoping to learn new ways of living within the context of modern technology and the changes that will ensue.

But I can't spend fifty-two weeks each year in these classes. I need companionship right where I am, right where I spend most of my time. And this need continues. We all need to find similar-minded people in order to feel comfortable and understood.

My prayer for you is that a support group that will be the springboard for interacting with other widows. There will certainly be times of loneliness, but with a network of support, your lives will be far richer. Of course your ultimate support is the Lord himself who promised, "Surely I am with you always, to the very end of the age" (Matt. 28:20).

SEVEN

Memories

Each of us has our own memories. Some are good. Some are less than good. When we say we're dealing with our memories, we mean that we're facing our yesterdays for what they mean to us today so we can get on to our tomorrows.

Maybe your husband died at home. For the months preceding his death, you knew it was going to happen. Toward the end, you may have called hospice to help out. But he still died there in your home. Do you still "see" the medical apparatus brought in by the hospice nurses? Does the aura of illness still linger in the house? Is it difficult for you to go into the room where he died?

Maybe your husband died in the hospital. A short time after my husband died in the emergency room at our local hospital, I received a call that a member of our church had been taken to that same emergency room. Several of us got together and immediately went there to be with her.

I entered the emergency ward and walked past the exact room where Earl had died. I shook my head as if to shake out the emotional memories of what had happened there. Then I went on down the hall to where our friend was. I found myself concentrating on her as I held her hand and tried to reassure her that everything was going to be all right. My friends and I prayed with her and she smiled weakly.

Several of the same nurses were there the night my husband died. I kept seeing them pass by the open door of my friend's room. As we were leaving, one of those nurses looked at me and asked, "Are you all right? We've all been worried about you." I replied, "I'm fine." Later on I wished that I'd finished that "fine" statement with this reminder from Philippians 4:13, "I can do everything through him who gives me strength."

Some memories are very painful, as Rainey, recently widowed, discovered. Her husband was an author who found it impossible to focus on his writing at home. So the two of them chose to rent a small cabin for him in a secluded area miles from their home where he could write without distraction. Working with a peaceful view of a running brook and deep, tranquil woods helped him concentrate on his writing.

This arrangement—he at the cabin and she remaining at home—worked well except for her bouts of loneliness. He completed and sold several books. As the royalties began to come in, it helped make some of their long periods of separation seem worthwhile.

He became almost obsessed with getting the next manuscript ready, and the next, and the next. He went to his cabin more and more frequently, staying for longer times. She never worried about this until one day there was a knock on the front door. Two uniformed police officers were there. The look on their faces told her immediately that something was wrong. They informed her that an intruder had surprised her husband and hit him over the head with a blunt instrument. He was killed instantly.

So she was a widow left alone with mixed memories of what their life had been. Some memories brought up anger. Whenever she passed the bookshelf and saw the books he'd written, it reminded her sadly of their long periods apart. Now, as a widow, those times of separation from her husband had become permanent. In her newly widowed state, she found it hard to recall which book was the last he wrote. What was he working on when he was killed? She swallowed hard every time as she tried to forgive the murderer of her husband.

Some memories spur us to go on. Nita and her husband finally accomplished the dream of owning a fast-food restaurant. Despite the tiring work and the long hours, they thoroughly enjoyed it because they were doing it together. This went on for several years until his untimely death. She decided she'd keep the restaurant. After all, they had wanted this for so many years. She just knew he'd want her to continue as long as she could. She hired extra help to fill the void knowing she couldn't possibly work the combined hours the two of them had put in. She'd come in early and stay late. As she worked, she could almost feel her husband's strength spurring her on. Memories of the good times they'd shared filled her mind.

Your memories may go back to when you first met your husband. It's good to recall those times when you and he were just getting to know each other. You may recall the place where you went on your first date, the songs you enjoyed dancing to, your first kiss, or the first time you realized that he was "the one." Those were good memories, but our memories change, as do our aspirations.

As the years go on, circumstances and things may happen that bring back less than perfect memories for you. Perhaps there were some unresolved issues between you. Maybe you secretly or overtly wished you had never married him. Those kinds of memories may be extremely painful to you at this vulnerable time in your life. Blending them all together—good and bad experiences—are what made you who you are today. Now that you're alone, you may find that your memories remind you of those experiences in some of the oddest ways.

Louise was an older widow. She and her husband had had a very special relationship. They had married late in life. He called her his "Beautiful Princess." When he developed a heart condition, she was devastated. The doctors gave no hope when he had the first attack, and in a few days he was gone.

Just as she was wrestling with adjusting to her life without him, she noticed that her right leg was noticeably weaker than the left. A visit to her internist gave her the news that she had developed a form of palsy. The doctor told her that, no doubt, she would soon need to use a cane in order to walk at all.

In time her facial muscles began to sag. As she looked at herself in the mirror, she thought of how important her looks were to her husband. The memories of those days were sweet. The reality of today was not so sweet. She tried to think positive thoughts and be glad for the days they did have when her health was still intact. In a peculiar sort of way she was glad that he didn't live to see his "Beautiful Princess" with a distorted face and a walking cane. Looking up toward heaven she hoped there was some sort of filter so that those in glory couldn't see the challenges their survivors had to deal with.

Some widows have to deal with the memories of a flawed marriage. Kay had endured her husband's numerous affairs. It seemed that he no sooner got over one relationship than he was out looking for another one. He acted as if he were trying to recapture his youth again by dating. She endured it as long as she was able to, and then they separated. He moved out, leaving her and their children in the family home. Occasionally he would call her and suggest they try to reconcile. She told him she would only consider it if he sought professional counseling. In time, he missed the children so much that he agreed to seek help.

After weeks of meeting with the therapist, they decided to try reconciliation for the children's sake. It was awkward at first. There were so many negative memories. On the other hand, he didn't seem at all fazed by what had happened. His behavior was still similar to that of an adolescent. Then one day he told the therapist that he kept hearing a ringing in his head. No matter what he did, the noise was still there. A short time later, he developed excruciating headaches and the therapist suggested he seek medical advice. A barrage of tests brought them unexpected news. He had an inoperable brain tumor.

From then on his health deteriorated rapidly. Her memories of how much he'd hurt her and their relationship were partly obliterated as she used every bit of energy to care for him. But, within a year he was gone. In retrospect she began to realize that the adolescent behavior he had exhibited was probably due to the tumor that had been growing, undetected, in his brain for a long time. That helped her through her grief and her adjustment to her new season of life, widowhood.

During this period of adjustment to your new life, you might hear a song that you both liked that makes you reflect back. You may even smile a little as you reminisce. You may see a show on television that you used to watch together and be reminded of him. And then you think, *He really liked this episode of that show.* But then you wonder, *Did he ever see that episode or did he die before that?* Your memories tend to get mixed up while you're in the grieving process. Those mixed-up memories can be with you long after the grief has passed and make you think that you're going crazy. We've already established the fact that you're not going crazy. Many widows have had those same mixed-up feelings.

When you see a car on the road just like the one he drove, your heart skips a beat . . . and then you remember.

When my husband died, just seeing his car in the driveway was extremely painful for me. My best friend took it and parked it in her driveway, which kept it out of my sight until I could sell it to another friend who lived in another county.

For years my husband and I grew Christmas trees. They were so much a part of my life that I still wonder if I will ever get over feeling sad when I see, smell, or feel a Christmas tree. They trigger in me of both good and not so good memories

Mondays are another trigger to my memories. Earl died on a Monday evening. For a long time afterward, each Monday was a terrible day of the week. When I see the numbers 911, I remember dialing that number. I remember the eternity it took for them to ask all their questions when all I wanted to scream at them was, "Just get here!"

Even today when I see an ambulance with its lights flashing, I remember the one that took him away to the emergency room. On television or in the movies, I see them performing CPR on a patient and I remember. I see doctors in white coats and I remember them coming to tell me they were sorry. And then I think that was years ago.

What were we doing before that time?
What about our last anniversary together?
His last birthday?
When was the last time we made love?

I watched the videotape of our last Christmas together—all the children, the in-laws, the grandchildren, and us. It was all so idyllic. Would any of us have reacted differently if we'd known it would be his last Christmas, or the last time his children would see their father? Memories—good and not so good.

I look through my closet and think: *Did he ever see that dress? Oh no, that's right, I bought that for the funeral. But what is there of my wardrobe that he did see? How much of me is now the new me? New hairstyle? New makeup? New attitude?*

Have you had similar experiences of these mixed-up memories and feelings? *Was that before or after he died that that current event happened? Did he live to see his favorite team win the Super Bowl?* Will you ever stop saying: "My husband used to," or "We used to."

Before we get in the habit of moaning about those memories, we need to look at them in the proper perspective. Our memories can be a comfort to us of what once was. One day we'll recall those times without intense longing, because: "The former things have taken place, and new things I declare; before they spring into being I announce them to you" (Isa. 42:9).

The former things are gone. They're the foundation we'll now build upon. But look again at what we're promised in the Scriptures. New things will spring into being. We're assured of that.

So our task as believers in God is to tuck away those memories deep within our hearts where they belong, as part of what once was, and look to what he has planned for us— what will be.

EIGHT

Finances

Y ou've heard those clichés about money:
"It talks."

"It makes the world go round."

"It's the root of all evil."

But in reality, the Scripture says, "The love of money is a root of all kinds of evil" (1 Tim. 6:10).

"Okay," we say. "We don't exactly love money. It's just that we need it for those incidental things like food, clothing, and shelter, to say nothing of college tuition and retirement."

Sarah's family came from a long line of pastors. Money had been a constant concern to them as she was growing up. Although they always had enough for the basics of life, there was never enough money for extra things. Her teeth could have benefited from braces, but a pastor's salary just couldn't afford them. They knew they were doing what they had been called to do, yet sometimes it was difficult. The family lived in houses owned by the various churches her father pastored. When he retired, her parents moved into a modest retirement home owned by their denomination. So when Sarah married a pastor, she assumed that her life would follow a path similar to that of her parents. However, the philosophy of their denomination had changed by that time. Instead of providing housing owned by the church, pastors were encouraged to purchase their own homes. And salaries were increased, accordingly, to help accomplish this.

When Sarah's husband died, she at least had a home to call her own, but she wondered how she could manage without his salary. She sought advice from others and learned that by taking a part-time job she would be able to keep her home. She worked twenty hours a week in a local Christian bookstore to augment her income. Another benefit of working was that it forced her to get out of the house and interact with other people.

She found, as many of you have found, that two cannot live as cheaply as one. Once there were two incomes, but now there is only one. Even with insurance, widow's benefits, or social security, your income has probably changed.

My income changed dramatically when my husband died. For twenty years, I'd been working in private Christian schools. In this type of work I did not earn much money, but my husband did in his consulting business. He always told me that he'd make the money so that I could continue to develop these Christian schools into the best they could be. In this way, he felt he was making a contribution to the work of the Lord.

This was all fine while he was alive, but then one day he was gone. I found that I was not only outside of his spiritual covering, but of his financial covering as well. Many times, I asked myself, *What am I going to do now?*

You may have asked yourself this question as well. What do you do about it? You have to go on, but how?

Evelyn's husband had the gift of giving. Each week he'd put a generous and consistent amount into the offering plate at church. Although she was grateful that he was able to do that, she realized after his death she could not keep up that practice. At first she felt a little guilty about her meager offerings. But then she remembered the parable Jesus told about the widow's mite. It was comforting to know she was doing all she could for now. Maybe later, things would be better, but for now she gave what she could.

A first rule of widowhood should be: *Don't be in a hurry.*

That rule applies to many facets of your life. It's an especially good idea to take your time regarding your finances. Before you jump headfirst into the world of high finance, you probably need to start at the beginning. There are legal issues that surround a death. There may be probate costs surrounding his will. You may need to look into putting the vehicle title and/or insurance in your own name—and money is probably involved.

Before panic sets in, make a list and prioritize the various aspects of your situation. If you feel you're still too fragile to do this, find a trusted friend to help you think things through. Maybe another widow who's been in this situation longer than you have could help you. Whatever you do, don't automatically ask your relatives for advice. They're too personally close to you and the situation.

Your local library or bookstore has books on money management and finances just for women. Check out the business channels on the television. If you don't understand everything they're talking about, that's okay. You're just learning. Remember it takes time to learn and understand. Keep listening and keep watching. Take notes to remind yourself of items you want to know about.

When you have ideas on your finances in order, according to the urgency of each, begin to tackle one thing at a time. You'll probably find relief when you see the list laid out in an orderly fashion. Remember the analogy in chapter 5 about eating a whole elephant? When you accomplish a task and can cross it off the list, there's a great feeling of accomplishment. And a feeling of accomplishment is what you need right now.

One of the first items on your list may be your bank account. Was your checking account a joint account? Are there money market accounts or certificates of deposit (CDs) that are in both of yours names or just his? If you can't answer these questions right now, that's okay. That's what customer service representatives at banks are for. Make an appointment to speak with one of them. Listen, take notes, and think about your options. Proceed according to your needs. Perhaps it would be more advantageous for you to hold those CDs until they mature. And when you decide what's best, then just do it!

You should explore ways to do your banking for the least amount of money possible. Call several banks. Get information on their fees for various accounts and write all the information down. Then you can compare and decide what is best for you and do it. Don't fret about hurting feelings. This is strictly business and you need to gather all the facts you can so you can look out for yourself.

Marilyn loved to watch television. She became enchanted by the commercials, which showed how easy, and *risk-free* day trading could be. "Buy low and sell high" was their claim. It sounded good to her. She felt she needed more money and this seemed like an easy way to get it.

She had a huge sum of money from an insurance policy on her husband's life, so she called a day trading company that advertised they could help her make money. She placed half of the money with this company, fully expecting to hear that it had doubled in value in a very short time.

But each month, as she looked at the reports of the account, the amounts kept getting smaller. When she called the company, she was told, "These things happen." When she realized her money had shrunk to 75 percent of what she had put into it, she pulled out of the program. She looked at the balance in her bankbook and wondered how she could have been so trusting and so blind. She kept telling herself that at least she had 75 percent left. She then sought out wise counsel from several persons and firms on what to do from then on.

Rose was another widow who had a large sum of money from an insurance policy. She had never had much money before, so she felt rich. She went on frequent spending sprees. She bought things, frequently, for all the family—generally useless items. And of course in a short time that *fortune* had shrunk.

If you are fortunate enough to have a *fortune,* or what the world perceives to be one, you may find yourself inundated by people with all sorts of ideas on how to invest it. Arlene was rather flattered to be asked out to dinner by a friend. He took her to a nice restaurant. During the meal, he kept the conversation light and entertaining. They chatted through the soup, the salad, the entrée, and the dessert. It wasn't until the second cup of after-dinner coffee was poured that he told her about a perfect plan for the two of them to invest in and get rich together.

His moneymaking idea was to buy rundown houses. Together they would restore them, and then sell them to low-income families. He spoke of huge profits. His green eyes were so intense as he talked. She could see the zeal he had for this project. She thought of the money they could make, and how this project could help others. She was very tempted to say, "Let's do it." Instead, she told him she would think it over. Arlene remembered some advice her father had given her a long time ago, "Give yourself three days to consider a project. If it still seems right, it may be just what you're looking for." She thought about it for three days and then for three more. Finally, she decided it wasn't for her. The next time he called and wanted to get together, she was intentionally busy.

Another thing to consider is, that as a widow, you may have inherited some money that your children feel is part of their inheritance. Perhaps they worry that they will not receive what is due them. Keep in mind that this money was left to you to care for your needs now. The bottom line is you need to be taken care of right now, and there will be time later to consider the next generation's needs.

When you were married, did you have a budget? Did you stick to it? Does that budget need to be changed now in light of what has happened? Make a list of your monthly expenses: rent, mortgage, insurance, food, etc. Then look at the income you can count on each month. If it's more than your expenses, you're fine for now. But if it's the other way around, you may need to make some adjustments. Keep an eye on your cash flow.

Some financial advisors suggest that everyone, widowed or not, needs to closely scrutinize their cash flow. One method is to write down everything you spend in a two-month period no matter how significant or insignificant you may think it is. At the end of this time, categorize what you spent. Most people find ways to save money when they see examples of frivolous spending. Advisors suggest this practice be done twice a year.

Maybe, because you don't have much money, you never thought of yourself as needing a financial advisor or a financial plan. But we all need a plan no matter how great or small the amounts we have to work with. In fact, when your finances are smaller, it's even more imperative to plan wisely about making your money do the most for you.

And don't let the words *estate planning* intimidate you. Now, more than ever, you need to have the most effective financial plan you can find to help you get your affairs in order. Connie prepared for her future by taking out an insurance policy that would cover nursing homes costs should she ever become unable to care for herself. She felt it was an excellent way to protect herself, and her children, from unexpected financial expenses in the future.

A good financial advisor can help you identify solutions tailored to your particular situation. The money spent for that advice could be one of the best investments ever made for you and your children. If you feel you can't afford professional help, there are Christian financial advisors who can help. Frequently their charges are on a sliding scale. Tune into your local Christian radio or television stations to see what advice you can glean from them.

I've listened to numerous presentations by financial planners. Each one seems to have their own agenda when it comes to widows. Although their advice may differ, I have learned a lot from them. Sometimes I follow their advice, but usually, I take time to think about it. I'm certain that I've annoyed some of them. In fact, one man left my house in a huff after I turned down his financial plan. He shouted at me from the driveway, "Ok, so you don't want to take care of yourself. What do I care?"

Don't cave into pressure. When, and if, you feel that you are ready to invest, remember the rule: *take your time!*

Well-meaning people may come to you with great ideas and hot tips. Be careful. Beware of the *Ides of Widowhood*! Study, listen, and learn. If their ideas still seem right for you, sit down and think about them some more. Still seem right? Then go ahead and do it!

On the other hand, if you want to try your hand at investing in mutual funds, stocks, or bonds, get the best advice you can find. Then sit down and think about what you want to do before jumping.

If you're afraid today, because of your financial situation, that's to be expected. There is only you now to make all those decisions. If you wonder some days where the next dollar is coming from, look to the Wealthy Provider who is caring for you through all of this. In Psalm 50:10, you're assured that your God owns the cattle on a thousand hills. Do you think that God would let his daughter down in any area, even the area of finances?

When you find yourself worrying about your finances, get on your knees and thank your heavenly Father for his provision for you, in all things at all times. And remember: "My God will meet all your needs according to his glorious riches in Christ Jesus" (Phil. 4:19).

NINE

What About Sex?

Your husband is gone, so your sex life is over. If you're a healthy, red-blooded female, this could cause problems for you. One of my dear friends was widowed a few months after I was. She commented to me, "Jan, how do you stand it? My husband and I were so physical!" Dear sisters, have you ever asked yourself, "How do I stand it?" Do you find it difficult even to walk through the men's department in large stores?

Pat worked at a large bookstore. She really enjoyed meeting customers and helping them find just the book they were looking for. She was always glad when she was assigned to the children's section, because she had several grandchildren. When she had a free moment, she would go through the stacks of books planning what she'd buy for them.

At the end of the day, however, she was often assigned to straighten up the store in preparation for the next day. She'd frequently find that she'd been assigned to work in the section containing books on sex. It was difficult to shelve those books and try to make them look good.

Straightening up the magazine section was another challenge. It was hard enough to keep the current events magazines in order, but it was extremely difficult for her to have to go through the "adult" section. She'd almost close her eyes as she forced herself to do her job. All those books and magazines were screaming reminders to her of how her sex life had been altered by the death of her husband.

Widows have faced their changed sexual lives in various ways. Alice, who claimed to be a Christian, said, "If I found the right man, I'd definitely consider a sexual relationship with him." This statement shocked her friend Glenda, who was with her. But over the years, her friend saw this was more common than she had once thought.

Rae chose to go away on frequent trips with her "significant other." Her rationale for this was the assumption that everyone else was doing it, so why not her? It was exhilarating when they went to exotic places together. In a way, each trip was like a honeymoon. They even used their own name when traveling together. When a friend asked her if that was a problem, she replied that many women don't change their last names when they marry, so who would know the difference? Besides, this way she had someone to travel with, and the depth of their relationship was no one's business but their own. Over the objection of her children, she shrugged and said, "That's just the way it is." She accused them of not caring about her happiness.

Ethel not only traveled with her male companion, but they also lived together in her house. When asked about it, her answer was, "I'd lose my Social Security and my late husband's pension if I remarried. I just can't afford to do that. Besides, what harm is there in what we're doing? We're not hurting anyone else."

Adrienne found it difficult seeing her friends either happily married or living with their male companions. She almost cringed visibly every time she saw a husband putting his arm lovingly around his wife, or a couple looking knowingly at each other. A solution that worked for her was to volunteer in a rural area where many low-income families resided. She did this several times each year. She loved to bring gifts to the children—clothes they needed or books their parents could not afford. With each gift she included a card to tell these children they were loved. The hugs and kisses she received from these children were a substitute for the lack of love she felt in her life.

Let's get personal now.

Do you miss having your husband put his hand on your knee with a reassuring physical touch that translates into, "We're okay, baby, because we're in this together?" Does your bed seem terribly empty now? Once it was a place of pleasure. Now there is just you, alone—without him—alone with your memories. If sleeping in the same bed is too painful, try changing rooms. Often widows find great comfort in sleeping in the same bed where their husband slept, snuggling into that spot.

In his infinite wisdom, the Lord made each of us different. So, if you feel comfortable sleeping where you did before or not sleeping there, either is okay. Do what is best for you as the Lord leads you. Be sure to read the Bible and listen to the Lord's directions, knowing that he understands your celibate state. Time will help, even in the area of your sexual life.

Daily, you face reminders that sexual activity is rampant today. The media is a primary source of this. Sex, it seems, is everywhere you look. Unless you plan to hole up in an ice igloo in the middle of Antarctica, you'll be inundated with sexual images. What is the solution?

Well, sexually suggestive programs on television can be changed with a wonderful device called the remote control. See a program that bothers you? Use that remote, and zap it! If the next channel displays the same, zap that one too. If this doesn't help, then turn off that TV set. Go to the kitchen for a soda or outside for a breath of cool, fresh air. Then come back inside, perhaps choosing to read a book or magazine. Sexual content can also be a problem here though, so make sure you stick to Christian novels and spiritual topics.

If reading Christian material still doesn't help, then seek other ways to meet unfulfilled needs. One way might be to listen to sermon tapes. After Earl died, I found a tape on singleness. It was primarily addressed to people who'd never been married, and it's main point urged abstinence before marriage. The gist of the message was if you hadn't tasted sex, then you wouldn't crave it. Fine! But what about those of us who have had sexual relations in marriage, and now, through no fault of our own, are suddenly single again?

It took great restraint for me not to stand up and shout at the pastor on that tape. Not that he would have heard me or cared anyway. I wanted to shout, *Why don't you ever address the needs of widowed people? You don't care about us at all. You're safe and secure in your marriage, so, of course, you wouldn't care about us.*

Some, who aren't widowed, may question such an intense reaction, but those of you faced with the same situation surely understand. And there's Someone else who understands. He tells us to: "Delight yourself in the LORD and he will give you the desires of your heart" (Ps. 37:4).

Trish didn't delight in the Lord. Her story began when she joined a Friday night women's bowling league. She thought it would be a good way to get out of the house and be around other people—something to help take her mind off the fact she was now alone. One evening, she noticed a tall, dark-haired man bowling in the adjacent lane. Between frames, she chatted with him. She liked his droll sense of humor and the way he noticed things about her. She saw him whenever she came to bowl. One night, he invited her out for a drink after bowling. And that started a relationship that did not honor the Lord.

Trish found that she could hardly wait to see this man every Friday. They continued to go out each week. Over time, they began to meet in the afternoon before bowling. Sometimes it was awkward to talk in public places, so he suggested they go to her apartment. She felt totally secure with this man, so she agreed.

Soon they were involved in a passionate sexual relationship. They would meet in the afternoon, go bowling, and then spend time alone together afterward. Trish wondered why he could only see her once a week. Finally, when she could stand it no longer, she asked him about it. His answer rang in her ears, as he told her he was married. He tried to soften the blow by saying his wife did not understand him.

She felt like kicking herself as she thought about how often that line was used in movies and novels. It was difficult for her to admit she was the "other woman." But whenever she tried to break it off, she found she couldn't resist the pleasures of their relationship.

Eventually, this man divorced his wife and married Trish. However, she was still haunted by the thought that she had been responsible for the breakup of a marriage. She'd allowed herself to focus on her own selfish desires, instead of placing them before God and asking his will in the matter.

When you focus on the Lord, and him alone, those desires for "what was" will be lost in the glory of seeking his will. When you yearn for what's gone, or when you yearn for a new love, you need to be assured that God will lead the way when it comes to your best interests. Do as the psalmist says and "delight in the Lord."

Don't fall prey to the world's telling you how to fulfill your desires. Secular counselors may tell you, "Do whatever gratifies you. After all, you're an adult. Choose for yourself. There are plenty of options."

Beware of the books written by psychologists who purport to know what is best for you. I read one that encouraged the reader to keep their sexual life active. The author reasoned, that if you didn't remain sexually active, you wouldn't be able to function successfully later on when you are in a relationship.

When I read my Bible, I find that the Lord promises he is more than able to take care of his people in all areas of their lives. In Joel 2:25 he tells us, "I will repay you for the years the locusts have eaten." I thank God that he can overcome the "locusts" of widowhood. If it's true that celibacy could cause problems later on, surely the Lord will erase that situation and bless you for your obedience to his Word.

As Christians, we're called to seek holiness in all areas of our lives. As widows, this may appear difficult, but with God's help we can pursue the holiness and purity he desires for us. Every day is a victory as we seek to be as pure as we can be in his sight. When the wiles of the world and the temptations of being alone are crashing in around us, we have help from the Lord: "May God himself, the God of peace, sanctify you through and through. May your whole spirit, soul and body be kept blameless at the coming of our Lord Jesus Christ" (1 Thess. 5:23).

TEN

Dating and Remarriage

When you're newly widowed, the mere thought of remarriage may be completely foreign to you. Others may think that they know what's best for you. A very good friend of mine was greeting people at the viewing for her husband. Several well-meaning friends said to her, "You're young. You'll marry again!" We can only wonder how that pierced her grieving heart and the hearts of her three sons as they stood there watching their now single mother at the casket of their father!

Those friends meant well. Others have said that to me. "Jan, I'm praying that you'll meet someone."

It seems that everyone is eager to get us out of our present situation, while we're doing our best just to cope.

We may be thrust into situations we're not quite ready for at a time when we're the most vulnerable. For example, several weeks after my husband died, I learned that a man I knew, a high school sweetheart whom I'd once seriously considered marrying, was widowed at almost the same time that I was. He still lived in our hometown, while I lived some distance away. I was tempted to get in touch with him because he'd never be able to find me under my married name.

So I went to the beach, for an afternoon, where I could be alone with my thoughts. I always found this atmosphere soothing to me. I asked the Lord to tell me what I should do. He gave me two answers. The first was "No, I don't want you to contact him." And the second was these words: "Learn to be content in any and all situations."

Violet had gone for a month-long visit to her married daughter's home in another state. Her daughter mentioned that she had recently run into a man who once lived in their hometown, and she had taken the liberty of inviting him to dinner one evening while her mother was visiting. When Violet saw this man, she immediately recognized him as a basketball player who had played basketball with her older brothers at their high school. He explained that his wife had died a few years earlier. It wasn't long before he and Violet began seeing each other. She changed her plans and extended her visit, not once but twice. In a few months, they decided to marry. They both realized this was not a chance meeting; they should be together for as long as the Lord allowed.

Just as the Lord sent what was best for that widow, he will, in his infinite wisdom, send what he knows is best for you. If you have reached the point where you feel you're ready to date and perhaps remarry, there are some things you should consider.

You're a different person now than you once were. Maybe the situations you've encountered as a single woman have made you more independent. Maybe they've made you more skeptical.

For the sake of argument, let's say that you are ready to consider having another man in your life. How do you go about meeting someone? Would you consider being part of an internet chat room? I've done it occasionally using a code name known only to me. The people I chat with are of varying ages. It's fun to be an encourager to high school students who use these rooms for a diversion after hard days at school. I've never used chat rooms as a way to seeking dates, but I've heard of others who've met their mates this way. But, as in all areas of getting back into the dating field, be extremely cautious.

This definitely holds true if you are tempted to place your profile in a personal ad. You've probably noticed the abundance of these ads in the newspapers and on the internet. There have been successful marriages as a result of these ads. This may be one way to meet people, but be careful.

Karen heard about dances being held in her area for Christian Singles. The attire was dressy/casual, so she bought a new dress and shoes. She used the best skills she knew for applying just the right amount of makeup. Then she got into her car, headed for the hotel where the dance was being held, and swallowed hard as she got out of the car. She purchased a ticket at the door and went into the ballroom. Circular tables were all around the room. A cursory glance showed her that many of these tables were already fully occupied with groups of men and women chatting and laughing almost feverishly. She finally noticed a vacant seat at a table with several women. The ladies there were pleasant enough, but she couldn't help noticing that their eyes wandered as they checked out the men in the room. Next she noticed the men in the room spent most of their time socializing and dancing with the younger women. She stayed for a short time and then made up a "going to the powder room" excuse and drove home.

Hannah had no intention of trying to meet someone. She felt strongly about the needs that crisis pregnancy centers fill, so she decided to volunteer to help with the annual Walk for Life in her area. She made phone calls, sent out brochures, and spoke to several groups in preparation for the event. On the day of the Walk, she got there early to help set up. She was just trying to unfold the legs on a portable table when a man came up to her and said, "Please allow me to help you." As he bent over to unfold the table, she noticed his slightly balding spot on the top of his head that reminded her of the same balding spot her late husband had.

She thanked her benefactor and began to set out water bottles and granola bars for the walkers. When she turned around, he was there again.

"Is there anything else I can do for you?" he asked in a gentle voice.

"You could pull up a chair and help me distribute items to the walkers as they come by," she said.

"Gladly," he said and sat down beside her.

He asked if she had helped with the walks before. She told him that this was her first time, explaining that her husband had died eight months ago. He looked at her with astonishment. His wife had died at the same time. And so began a friendship, which blossomed into romance and two years later, marriage.

Let's assume you meet a man you'd consider dating. What criteria should you use? A widower would understand what you're going through, but make sure he's over his grief and is ready for another relationship.

Dottie had been widowed for eight years when she remarried. The man's wife had been deceased only a few months. After two years of marriage she realized her new husband wasn't finished grieving. They went through months of professional counseling to help him work out his grief.

Some states require premarital counseling for anyone applying for a marriage license. Those who have been married may scoff at this, and feel they don't need it, but when you consider the high divorce rate, even among Christians, you can see how vital it is to seek professional advice prior to remarriage.

When a friend of Olivia's learned that her fiancé was seventy-two, she asked Olivia sincerely, "What will happen if he becomes ill? You'll have to take care of him. It will be tough since you two haven't raised children together and built your lives together."

The widow thought about that for only a short time. True, he might become ill, and she would have to take care of him, but it didn't matter. The next time she saw him, she told him about her friend's concern, and she assured him, "If you ever do become ill, I will still love you and care for you."

Widows frequently have to learn how to handle the presence of the widower's children. Could they feel you're trying to take their mother's place or be a threat to their inheritance? Clara, who had recently married a widower, was delighted when his daughter introduced Clara to her friends as "my Dad's bride and my new Mom." She and her step-daughter have such a good relationship that her husband jokingly signs greeting cards to her with Dad and WSM (which stands for Wicked Step-Mother).

If the situation is reversed, will he be able to accept your children, especially if he's never been married? Could this cause problems for your children too? Perhaps they will feel as if you are trying to replace their father. Second marriages come with their own unique joys and problems, and there are more factors to consider than the first time around.

Consider this scenario also: suppose he is divorced. Does that change the situation? What does Scripture have to say about this subject? " 'I hate divorce,' says the Lord God of Israel" (Mal. 2:16). Is marrying a divorced man scripturally unacceptable for a widowed woman? In my opinion, these questions are best answered by thoughtful prayer and seeking the Lord's will. You can also seek guidance from a pastor or Christian counselor.

What if the man you're interested in is an unbeliever? We're told an unbelieving spouse is sanctified by the believer, but we're also warned in 2 Corinthians 6:14 not to be unequally yoked with an unbeliever.

Whether the man you consider marrying has been widowed, divorced, or never married, there are varying aspects to consider. For example, many attorneys recommend prenuptial agreements. It would be wise to study the subject for yourself and then make a decision based on what you've learned and how you both feel about it.

You may also need to check the community property laws in your state. Blithely entering into a marriage assuming that each person's assets will be retained separately is not a good idea. Sometimes state laws don't permit it, anyway.

When you do marry, will you keep your bank accounts separate or merge everything into one joint account? Should you keep your own name, hyphenate your name with his, or take his name? If you've had a career in your name, you may consider keeping that name for business purposes and use his name socially. All these are personal preferences that should be resolved before the wedding.

These are some of the questions you need to pray over and ask the Lord about. If you are seeing a man, how much control will you let him have over you? If you have been self-sufficient, would you feel stifled if he kept calling to check up on you? One widow, Bonnie, went on a vacation with several friends. When she returned home and checked her answering machine, she found that the man she'd been dating had repeatedly called all week because he was *so worried* about her. This was her clue to end the relationship.

Roxanne was dating a man her friends considered all wrong for her. She had a master's degree in Interior Design and was well known in her position. He was unemployed, living on welfare, and drifted from apartment to apartment after frequent evictions. From time to time he dated other women without telling her. In her heart, she knew her friends were right although she'd never admit it to them. However, her best friend could see that something was troubling her. She suggested that the two of them go to lunch at a quiet restaurant. There, as they enjoyed their salad and quiche, the friend asked her a direct question, "Do you really feel that he is good for you?" Roxanne looked down nervously. She arranged and rearranged the spoons beside her china plate. Finally, with tears welling up in her eyes, she looked up at her friend and said; "I'd marry anyone, even the wrong person, to keep from growing old alone."

You may be thinking by now that it's better to stay single rather than get into a situation that could be far worse. The apostle Paul says, "Now to the unmarried and the widows I say: It is good for them to stay unmarried, as I am" (1 Cor. 7:8).

Before you make up your mind to remarry or stay single, look to the Scriptures as your source of wisdom. One of the books in the Old Testament that can give you some insight into a widow remarrying is the book of Ruth. This book has always been very significant to me. My mother's name was Ruth. Just like the Ruth of the Old Testament, she was widowed when she was very young. She had no children. She was alone. It was several years later that she became reacquainted with a man she'd known back in high school. They were married and had me. They were the parents the Lord had chosen for me.

When you look at the story of Ruth and her mother-in-law, Naomi, you can see with certainty how the Lord has a hand in all of our lives. We may think our lives are over. We may tell others to call us *Mara* (bitterness) as Naomi did, but the Lord has other plans for us. Look at what happened to Ruth. She became an ancestor of Jesus Christ himself.

Who knows what good things he has in store for you. The Lord God Almighty has a plan designed just for you. Rest in that and trust that whether widowed or married, you are loved by him "with an everlasting love" (Jer. 31:3).

ELEVEN

Coming to Grips with Your New Life

I've discovered that books and studies identifying the paths or stages of widowhood are right on target. The studies tend to classify the stages as years. My experience has been that these years can be literal years or they can span much shorter or longer times. Think of them as steps a widow goes through as she comes to grip with her loss. Experts say that the first year or stage of widowhood is numbness.

The first time I traveled after my husband died, I packed just my things. The plane ticket was just one, so I had my choice of a window or an aisle seat. I really didn't care. Friends volunteered to drive me to the airport and to pick me up when I returned.

When I was all ready to go, I picked up my suitcase. As I was struggling to get it down the stairs, I said to myself: *Well, it's only you now. You'd better get used to it.* When I look back on that, I'm amazed that I was so rational at the time. One thing I did after that was buy lighter luggage with wheels. My choice was a very feminine tapestry with flowers on it.

During the second year or stage I began to realize just what had happened. It's not that I hadn't known it before; it's just that the numbness started to wear off. I found I was better prepared to face my situation and make plans for getting on with my life.

Along about the third stage or year, I could look at myself in the mirror and say, "I know who I am. I'm no longer Mrs. Sheble. I am me. I am not part of a pair. I am who I am.

When you look through the Bible, you can find the story of one widow who spent her time of acceptance in glorifying the Lord. This widow's name was Anna (Luke 2:36-38). She was a young widow who'd been married only seven years. At the time of this story, Anna was eighty-four years old.

She'd spent all those years in the temple, fasting and praying. She was a prophetess. When Mary and Joseph came to the temple, "She gave thanks to God and spoke about the child to all who were looking forward to the redemption of Jerusalem" (Luke 2:38). Her sole purpose in life during the final fifty or so years of her life was to glorify God.

In addition to the pictures on my refrigerator of my grandchildren, I have a small sign that says,

IF GOD HAD A REFRIGERATOR, YOUR PICTURE WOULD BE ON IT.

I smile when I pass it imagining what God might say to someone who asks him about the picture. "That's my daughter. Isn't she beautiful? She's not here right now, but when she gets here, she'll be with me forever."

The Lord himself said, "When the dead rise, they will neither marry nor be given in marriage; they will be like the angels in heaven" (Mark 12:25).

You can rejoice in this and wait for that great day with anticipation. But in the meantime, here you are—widowed and alone. How you respond to that is completely up to you. You can go around sniveling and miserable, moaning about your situation, or you can look to Job who had more than his share of troubles. He says, after all his mind-boggling ordeals: "You will surely forget your trouble, recalling it only as waters gone by" (Job 11:16).

Dear sisters, let's face facts. This is the hand we've been dealt. We may have preferred another set of circumstances, but this is the place our heavenly Father has planned for each of us. "In him we were also chosen, having been predestined according to the plan of him who works out everything in conformity with the purpose of his will" (Eph.1:11). However difficult, we should look for the good that will come about, even from our tragedy.

One night, Amy had a dream. In it, she saw her husband and he told her that before his death, he had conspired with medical personnel to freeze his body. Now, years later, they had perfected the method to bring him back to life. He wanted to come back and take up where they had left off. In the dream, she told him that she had lived all these years without him, had become self-sufficient, and didn't think she could go back to their former life.

It was at this point that she woke up in a cold sweat. She got up and paced the floor. She turned on the lights and decided to make a cup of tea. As she sat at the kitchen table, she thought about what her dream could possibly mean. Surely it didn't mean that she yearned for her husband to return. She shook her head as she thought more about it. It was then that she realized that the most significant aspect of the dream was that she had become self-sufficient. She made peace with her loss and was headed toward her future.

Terry was a young woman who thought she knew what she wanted to do with her life. She planned to go to college, major in biology, and go to the mission field. After graduation, she returned to her hometown. Among her acquaintances was a much older man. He was a true Bible scholar. Her parents knew him well and respected him. He'd been part of the pastoral staff at her church and she'd listened to his teaching from the time she was a little girl. He also taught part-time at a seminary. She decided to enroll and take a class or two from him. That's when she learned he'd been widowed while she'd been away at college. She found herself looking forward to taking the classes he taught. His wisdom was the main thing that attracted her to him, but she soon found that she was being drawn to him romantically.

To her surprise, he was also attracted to her. They began meeting for coffee after class. At first they discussed the topics from the class sessions. She felt more and more drawn to him and could tell from the look in his eyes that he felt the same way. In one sense, it frightened her; but in another sense, she felt secure in their relationship.

In time they began to discuss what the next step might be in their relationship. Terry was twenty-three and he was sixty-seven. They both knew the probability of his dying much earlier and decided to pray about it separately. They each received the same answer—they should marry.

They decided he'd cut back on his teaching schedule, so they'd have more time together. He was often asked to preach in various locations around the world. This meant that they could travel to those places together. She learned so much from these experiences. And having him with her all the time meant they could discuss aspects of the Bible which she might never have understood without his knowledge.

They were together for ten glorious years, when he passed away. Terry was able to take care of the arrangements because they had discussed them beforehand. He and his first wife had pre-planned their funerals. Bravely, Terry sat through the memorial service and the interment and watched as her husband was laid to rest beside his first wife's grave.

Terry was okay with this. She knew that God was in control of everything. And as she got back into the limousine to leave the cemetery, she thanked the Lord for the years he'd given them. She had been given a blessing in him. Now she accepted his death.

She thought a lot about the preplanning he and his first wife had done. Have you thought about this? Or, are you where I was? My husband and I never made definite plans. So when the aftermath of his sudden death was over, one of my initial thoughts was, " I need to look into this."

Since that time, I've made prearrangements including transportation insurance if I should die while on a trip. My children have the toll-free phone number for the company where I purchased it. It's all part of my coming to grips with my own mortality.

You, too, need to accept what has happened and get on with your life. One dictionary definition of *acceptance* is, "To take what is offered or given willingly, to receive favorably, to approve."

Carole and her husband had been married almost fifty years. Six months before their anniversery, they planned a celebration for the big day. They rented a hall and paid a caterer. Carole bought a new dress for the occasion and her husband bought a new suit. He looked so handsome in it.

But, two months before the party, he had a heart attack and was gone. He was buried in that new suit. As she viewed him she said to herself, "He's still handsome in that suit." Before the casket was closed, she asked the funeral director to give her her husband's wedding ring.

After the funeral, she was determined to continue with the plans for the anniversary celebration. Her children couldn't understand why she wanted to do this, but she knew. She took her husband's wedding ring to a jeweler who fashioned it into a heart. He attached it to a gold chain.

On the day of the fiftieth anniversary party, she wore her new dress and his wedding ring on the gold chain. She celebrated with her family and friends and they all rejoiced that he'd been a part of their lives for so long.

Acceptance doesn't mean cowering in a corner, licking your wounds, and saying, "Woe is me!" Acceptance means having a favorable attitude and approval of the situation. Remember God could have chosen to let your husbands live. But what if his choice had been for your husband to spend the rest of his life, years perhaps, in a coma with no hope of recovery? Would that have been better or worse than his death?

When you can look at life philosophically, it helps you understand that God does know best. He made you. He understands and knows with infallible wisdom what is best.

So, each widow is then called to look into the mirror and say: *I know who I am. I am a person in my own right. I can make my own wise decisions. I can trust my own judgment.*

This is certainly reassuring, but it can also be scary!

My husband and I talked things over in our marriage and my opinion counted. Many times, he would opt to do what I suggested. But the final decision was always his. Now, as I think back on it, I realize that I was probably glad to let him have the responsibility, so that I didn't really have to think about it.

If I didn't have responsibility, then it was not my fault if something went wrong as a result of his decision. I further realize that since he's no longer here, I have no one to blame for a mistake but myself. But I do have the independence now to make my own decisions and yes, even my own mistakes. After studying, praying, and asking the Lord to grant wisdom, I have the confidence to accept his answer and act responsibly.

I find that I feel more confident. I definitely am more independent now that I am a widow. And although I seek professional advice in many areas of my life, I trust my own judgment now.

When you work on having confidence in yourself, you will be better able to cope and be less fearful. Then you can apply these words from Job 11:18: "You will look about you and take your rest in safety."

TWELVE

Seeking God's Will for the Rest of Your Life

You've gone through the intense fire of bereavement. You've trod upon the burning coals of grief. Now all you see are ashes. What should you do with those ashes? Isaiah 61:3 says that the Spirit of the Lord will "Bestow on them a crown of beauty instead of ashes."

Does your life look like a forest that's been ravaged by fire? What is left? What good can possibly come out of this?

When you look closely at the black, sooty soil of your life, you'll soon see small sprigs of green pushing their way up through the ashes. There is rebirth even in the midst of hopelessness. And as those sprigs grow, many of them will burst forth in vibrant hues of yellow, orange, or red flowers. It's as if the Lord is proclaiming to the world that he will overcome. And you, too, can survive and even overcome widowhood. And the Lord is eager to bestow that crown of beauty upon you.

When Michele was growing up, her parents favored her older brother. He was the smart one. She was the chubby, redheaded, freckled, *dumb* one. She carried this lack of self-worth into her adulthood and throughout her marriage. She felt she wasn't as good as everyone else. She worked in the cafeteria at a local elementary school. She'd often look at the teachers and wish she was as smart as they were.

When her husband died, she found that he had a life insurance policy she hadn't known about. One of the teachers at the school suggested she think about enrolling at the local community college. This teacher offered to tutor her if necessary.

Michele enrolled in two basic courses the next semester. She discovered college was not as difficult as she'd imagined. After she finished her shift in the school cafeteria, she had plenty of time to study. Often, she'd go to the college library and immerse herself in reading about subjects she'd only dreamed of. A whole new world was opening up to her, and she was eager to learn. Her grades were good; she received an "A" in one class and a "B" in the other. This gave her the incentive to continue and she enrolled in more courses. In a few semesters, she'd earned an associate's degree.

Armed with this victory, and the encouragement of her teaching mentor, she decided to enroll at a state university that was within commuting distance of her home. In three years, she earned a bachelor's degree in elementary education. Michele was overjoyed when she was hired to be a teacher in the very school where she'd worked so long in the cafeteria. She has since gone on to get a master's degree.

Several former coworkers from the cafeteria asked her how she'd managed to complete school so successfully. She was able to tell them with confidence that she'd persevered and hadn't given up. She told them, "If I can do it, then any of you can as well." Michele did her best, and with the Lord's help, went on to have a productive, happy life.

When you find yourself accepting your status today in relation to your former life, you should start feeling much more comfortable and independent. Now what to do?

Along with this newfound independence may come the realization that you are freer than you have ever been in your life. In marriage, compromise and the needs of two people took precedence over any opportunities to think only of yourself.

Perhaps you've always wanted a pink bedroom with lace curtains on the windows. That was probably inappropriate when your husband was living. Now you're free to indulge your wants and needs, and yours alone. The only possible threat to your independence might come from your grown children when they insist you start carrying a pager so they can keep track of you.

Emily had always wanted to seek new adventures. She decided to learn to sail, and found a school in the Northeast that offered beginning classes in sailing. Imagine her delight when she was told they had sailing crews that were all female. With eagerness, she set about to learn the charts and tables used in sailing. She also learned teamwork as she and the other women experienced firsthand the delicate intricacies of manning a schooner or a windjammer.

Her first trips were taken only in the Northeast. Later, she made trips to the Caribbean and to the Mediterranean. She loved being out on the sailboat enjoying the smell of the salt air, listening to the sounds of the seagulls as they swooped overhead, and feeling the gentle ocean breezes on her face. It was wonderful having no one to answer to other than her crewmates. Thoughts of being accountable to her grown children were pushed from her mind as she concentrated on her tasks among the crews.

Dear sisters, when you think about it, the only person you're accountable to for the way you live your life is God. This was true all along, even though you may not have realized it until just now.

Flo was alone, widowed at the age of fifty. She was able to thank the Lord for it, in spite of her sorrow, and asked him what he would have her do with the rest of her life. The answer he gave astonished her. She was to go to Central America. When she asked for more specific instructions, there was only silence. *I guess I'll find out when I get there*, she told herself. She started to brush up on her high school Spanish and began making firm plans for the trip.

Upon her arrival in Central America, she knew immediately what the Lord had in mind when he sent her here. The people of the small village, where she found herself, lived in extreme poverty. Certainly, they needed material goods, but they also needed to know Jesus Christ even more. Remembering Jesus' words in John 21:18, "feed my sheep," Flo began contacting her home church and the church's denomination to secure funds to help these people.

She made regular trips home and shared her experience with others. She showed slides of the children with their large dark eyes, their tattered clothes, and their mothers cooking mush for every meal. Flo's pictures and stories of these people touched her church family, and they agreed to send the much-needed items back to the village with her.

One of these church members was a salesman for an over-the-counter drug manufacturer. He offered to donate products that were still usable, explaining that when the company redesigned packaging, they were left with a surplus of usable drug supplies that could not be sold in stores. They were always happy to give them to a worthy cause.

Flo's obedience to the Lord resulted in many of the church members, including widows and widowers, planning their own short-term mission trips to the little village. They started discovering exactly what was needed in order to be of service to the Lord for the remainder of their lives. Some helped build a church building, and then returned every year, thereafter, to help run Bible school for the children and to evangelize in the neighboring villages. Flo, after heeding the call of the Lord, now spends nine months out of every year living and working beside these people, only returning home long enough to solicit funds and other assistance for her Central American "family."

Just as Flo did, you also can look for ways in which to serve God and, through prayer, determine the path he's chosen for you. As you do, be careful not to let the advice of others, no matter how well intentioned, deter you from what you've heard the Lord say. Perhaps you will hear words such as these:

"I think you should.

"When my sister was widowed, she . . ."

"Think about yourself first."

Ask yourself: *What specific tasks would the Lord have me do?* There are as many answers to this question as there are widows. The Lord may call one widow to mentor younger women. He may call another to a praying ministry, and still another to _____ (fill in the blank as he speaks to you).

Perhaps he's calling you to help those in authority see the need for a ministry to widows. Many times the needs of the widowed are overlooked—something you may have experienced yourself. Even within the church, and Christian culture, the heartfelt needs of the widowed are largely ignored. You, too, could choose to turn a blind eye to their suffering, or make a difference by doing everything in your power to help address these needs.

If your church does not offer a program for the widowed, then start one yourself. You could even give it a catchy name like, "The Widow's Might." Just think of the impact this could have on these hurting people and for the church community at large. You could even consider branching out into the secular realm—another way to bring Christ's message to widowed people who do not know him.

Other support groups could be formed as an outgrowth of the original one. Groups for eating out, attending movies and sporting events, or even for traveling could be arranged. The possibilities of demonstrating Christ's love are truly endless.

Another great way to minister to the widowed is to involve the church singles—those who are single due to divorce or those who've never been married. Offer to educate them on your group's needs, and show them you're interested in their needs as well. Persuade them to become involved in your group and learn about being widowed. Approach the single's pastor, who is usually married, and offer to teach him how to be more sensitive to the needs of your group.

Just remember, when attempting to make changes of this magnitude, make prayer a priority and ask, "Lead me, O LORD, in your righteousness . . . make straight you way before me" (Ps. 5:8).

In the process, your own spiritual life will improve. Consider taking courses in secular topics, in order to keep your mind keen, and to better relate to unbelievers. Knowing something about their concerns will prepare you, all the more, to be an effective witness for Christ. God has given us a wonderful thing called the mind, and he expects us to use it for his glory. Certainly, a good way to do that is to continue learning.

Think, also, of the new person you're becoming as you serve others and learn about their special needs and concerns. Little by little, you'll see changes taking place within you and begin to recognize the differences between the old you and the new you. Widowhood presents its own unique challenges, and how you approach and adapt to it cause changes evident to all.

So if someone says to you, "My, you sure have changed?" You can reply, "I certainly have!"

It's true. You have changed. Walking through the fiery furnace of widowhood has reaped benefits in you that would not have been possible otherwise. Profound changes have taken place within you, and you'll find through it all you've learned to be content. Now you can say what Paul said so long ago, "I know what it is to be in need, and I know what it is to have plenty. I have learned the secret of being content in any and every situation, whether well fed or hungry, whether living in plenty or in want. I can do everything through him who gives me strength" (Phil 4:12, 13).

What lies ahead will be better than you ever dreamed. Think of your life as a house being built on the firm soil of the Lord. Thank him for this work he is doing in your life.

"'The glory of this present house will be greater than the glory of the former house,' say the LORD Almighty. 'And in this place I will grant peace,' declares the LORD Almighty" (Hag. 2:9)

Appendix A

Support Group Questions

SUPPORT GROUP QUESTIONS
CHAPTER 1
"He's Gone"

1. Were the words "he's gone" a relief, a shock, or a surprise to you? What was your reaction? Do you find yourself dwelling on those moments?

2. How were those first few days for you?

3. Who or what ministered to you and carried you through?

4. Do you feel you can now minister to a recently widowed person or do you need more time? Explain.

5. Do you have the assurance of your husband's salvation? If not, how can you seek the peace that passes all our human understanding?

SUPPORT GROUP QUESTIONS
CHAPTER 2
Immediate Plans

1. During those first few weeks, did you push yourself to be strong or did you allow yourself to show grief?

2. How did you react when you were "numb?" Did you weep, cry, or stay silent?

3. Did the thought of just running away from all that pain ever enter your mind? What was your response?

4. Did you have trouble getting rid of his belongings? Why do you think you cling to items that remind you of him?

5. How are you doing now with decisions? The day-to-day ones? The ones that could be put on hold for now?

SUPPORT GROUP QUESTIONS
CHAPTER 3
The First Year

1. Do you agree that the first year is the hardest? Why do you agree or disagree with this?

2. Was your first year a frenzied one or a continuation of your numbness?

3. How can you, as a widow, forget what is behind you and strain toward what is ahead?

4. If you've had feelings of incompleteness, how have you handled them?

5. What can make you complete?

SUPPORT GROUP QUESTIONS
CHAPTER 4
Regrets

1. What has helped you most in dealing with regrets?

2. It really is too late to make up for any mistakes you may have made in your relationship with your husband. Is anything unforgivable? Consider how sufficient your God is to cover it all.

3. Have you considered the "what ifs?" and then gotten down on your knees to thank the Lord for what he did grant you in your marriage? If not, why not?

4. What can you do to accept the infallible truth that the Lord understands your human frailty completely, with no reservations?

5. Do you trust the Lord to help you erase the negativity from any regrets you may have? Can you share some of those regrets with the group?

SUPPORT GROUP QUESTIONS
CHAPTER 5
Single Parenting

1. How do you approach the problem of worrying or concern? Make a list of those worries and concerns. Share with your group.

2. Have you considered your children's future? What concrete legal actions, or other steps, have you taken to assure their care if you don't survive long enough to raise them?

3. How are your children handling the loss of their father?

4. Where do you feel you can get the emotional support you need now as a single parent?

5. If your children are grown, how do you handle being a single mother or grandmother?

SUPPORT GROUP QUESTIONS
CHAPTER 6
Loneliness

1. When you feel lonely, what do you do? What are the ways that you've found work best for you?

2. Describe a time when you felt like a fifth wheel. How did you try to overcome it?

3. If you ever feel resentful that you're alone and it seems that no one else is, what do you do about it?

4. What might be some pros and cons of altering your living situation in an attempt to avoid loneliness?

5. Where have you found the best support as you adjust to being single?

SUPPORT GROUP QUESTIONS
CHAPTER 7
Memories

1. Does it seem that everything reminds you of your husband? Your loss? The way it happened? How do you deal with this?

2. Do you get confused in establishing when events occurred? Before? Or after? Can you accept the fact that you're not alone in this and that we've all had similar feelings? What do you think we can do about this?

3. With time, do you feel that the good memories outweigh the not so good ones or is it the other way around? Can you give examples?

4. Do you really feel that you're dealing with your memories or are they controlling you?

5. Do you still think daily of him and what was? Or are there times when you realize you're going on without a thought of him? If you do, how do you handle those times?

SUPPORT GROUP QUESTIONS
CHAPTER 8
Finances

1. Think about your financial situation before and after your husband's death. Do you feel it's better or worse than before?

2. If your Social Security or other benefits aren't sufficient, what can you do about it?

3. Have you developed a plan for your financial situation? If you can't do this on your own, have you sought professional advice? If so, from where?

4. Do you know with all your heart that your Heavenly Father owns the cattle on a thousand hills? Do you have confidence in him to trust that he'll care for you in all areas—even your finances? If not, what steps can you take to assure yourself of that?

5. The general rule is "take your time." Have you done that? Or have you chosen not to do anything for a long time? Can you think of remedies for this?

SUPPORT GROUP QUESTIONS
CHAPTER 9
What About Sex?

1. How have you handled the loss of your sex life?

2. Describe any sexually tempting situations where you could easily have given in. What did you do about it?

3. How does overcoming or not overcoming sexual temptation make you feel?

4. Do you think of yourself as sanctified?

5. Read Psalm 37:4. Can you really believe with your very being that the Lord will put the desires within you? Give some specific examples.

SUPPORT GROUP QUESTIONS
CHAPTER 10
Dating and Remarriage

1. How do the morals and practices of today appear to you? If you're frightened, why do you think you feel that way? If they don't bother you, why do you think this is so?

2. Would you consider remarrying? Why or why not?

3. Would you only consider a widowed or never-married man? Would you consider a divorced man? Give your reasons.

4. Have you been tempted to try to meet men? How?

5. Consider the biblical story of Ruth and Naomi. What message is there in this for you?

SUPPORT GROUP QUESTIONS
CHAPTER 11
Coming to Grips with Your Life

1. What stage or "year" of grieving do you feel you're in right now? Numbness? Realization? Acceptance?

2. Have you thought about the truth that in the eyes of the Lord, he has always seen you as single? How does that affect your thinking about your newly single status?

3. In what ways can you trust your own judgment to make decisions for yourself?

4. Have you reached the point where you can begin to see a rosy future ahead of you? If not, what steps can you make to begin looking for the positives in your life?

5. How do you feel as you view your situation today? How can you really accept that you'll dwell in safety because of the Lord Jesus Christ?

SUPPORT GROUP QUESTIONS
CHAPTER 12
Seeking God's Will for the Rest of Your Life

1. Now what? What are your plans for the future?

2. To whom do you feel accountable today?

3. How's your prayer life? Your study of Scripture?

4. Do you feel closer to the Lord or farther from him, now that you're widowed? Why do you think this is?

5. Write out your plan for diligently seeking the Lord's will for the rest of your earthly life.

Appendix B

Guidelines for Using This Book in a Group Setting

The purpose of a support group is to give courage, to help, and to comfort each other. Although there are various ways this can be accomplished, the following suggestions may help.

- Designate a leader. Leadership can be the responsibility of one group member, or can be rotated. A coleader can be helpful to the leader.
- Every member of the group should have her own copy of the support group book. Before each session, she should read the chapter for the week, underlining and taking notes as needed. A notebook is useful

for notetaking and to record questions and thoughts that come to mind. Each member should go over the questions for each chapter in preparation for the group meeting. This will not only make your sessions more meaningful, but will make future reference easier for you.

- The group size should be limited to eight to ten women. You may want to write the names and phone numbers of each group member in your notebook. Here again, this will make future reference much easier.

- Remember that a support group doesn't guarantee instant miracles. It does, however, pave the way for the Lord to work his healing and show his power.

- To be most effective, the support group should meet once weekly for twelve consecutive weeks, covering one chapter each week.

- To protect confidentiality and to build trust, we recommend that no new members be admitted after the second meeting. After that time, if others would like to join, help start a new group for them.

- Everyone in the group must agree not to talk to anyone else about what transpires during a session. Anyone who violates this agreement should be warned that such behavior could and should be cause for dismissal from the group.

- Set time limits for each session and adhere to them. Remember that each person's time is valuable.

- Keep in touch with your support group members during and even after the twelve weeks.
- Be available to provide leadership for future support groups, following these guidelines.
- Don't neglect the importance of individual and corporate prayer in the process of your healing and becoming the person God planned for you to be.

Appendix C

Points for Further Reflection

You've gone through the twelve chapters of this book. You may feel that many of your concerns have been addressed, but you still have questions. You wonder if you are the only one with such silly things to wonder about. Maybe others are more together than you are.

However, many widows still struggle with unanswered questions. We know that the Lord is in charge, yet we still wonder, "Why?"

When we reach that perfection known as Glory, where we will be with the Lord forever, we will gain some understanding. But while we are in the flesh we seek to comfort ourselves in knowing that the Lord God himself has said to us: "For my thoughts are not your thoughts, neither are your ways my ways" (Isa. 55:8).

The questions and statements you will find in this Appendix are typical of those I discovered as I talked with other widows. The answers are a combination of personal and other experience, study, and meditating on the word of God.

Before you even begin to delve into studying and poring over these points for further reflection, ask the Lord to open your heart so you will be ready to learn the truths he is so eager to share with you.

On the surface, portions of these questions may appear to be more "theological." Remember, the Lord gave you intellect. He expects you to think for yourself, to learn, to read, to ask questions, and to seek wisdom from him. You may find that as time goes by, you see things in a different light. That's okay. As you open your heart to the Lord you are growing in knowledge.

It's a good idea to discuss these questions with others. Your support group members are one source of understanding by discussing these items with them. Your pastor or an elder at your church may also be able to give you some insight. Whatever you do, pray for wisdom so you'll be open to what God has to say to you. Keep these words in your heart because, "We know that in all things God works for the good of those who love him, who have been called according to his purpose" (Rom. 8:28).

I'm really mad at God for taking away my husband. Does this mean I'm a bad person?

If you're mad at God right now that's probably a good thing. Before I'm accused of being too heretical, let me clarify what I mean by that. When you were widowed, you felt something very precious was taken away. Job says, "The LORD gave and the LORD has taken away; may the name of the LORD be praised" (Job 1:21). How can you be expected to praise a God who has taken away your husband? It's no wonder you might be mad at such a God. In fact this can be part of the healing process in your grief.

There have been persons who were so "into" their Christian faith, that they never questioned why the Lord chose death for their spouses. Then, when the trials of life got overly burdensome, they found that they should have gone through the process of grieving. They would have been better off if they had gotten mad. In this way they could truly accept what happened as the Lord's will.

You see it doesn't mean you're bad if you question or are angry with God. Remember who made you and who therefore understands even your most jagged emotions. "O LORD, you have searched me and you know me. You know when I sit and when I rise; you perceive my thoughts from afar" (Ps. 139:1, 2). He knows and cares for you deeply. He understands when or why you may be angry with him. As your Father, he loves you anyway. Do you stop loving your children or think of them as bad when they have their little bouts of temper tantrums or display anger at you? Then consider how the perfect parent, God, must think about you. He knows. He understands.

In time you will understand his perfect will. Your understanding of all these events may come while you are still here in the flesh or it may come when you reach glory. For "now we see but a poor reflection as in a mirror; then we shall see face to face. Now I know in part; then I shall know fully, even as I am fully known" (1 Cor. 13:12). What a magnificent time that will be when we comprehend all things.

But, in the meantime, while you're still here on earth, you need to seek peace in your life. It's okay to feel angry at the Lord for taking away your husband. However, don't let your anger become your focus and deter you from experiencing God's plan for your life.

Rather than harboring constant anger for what has happened, you are called to look ahead and ask the Lord what he wants for you. Say to him, "Teach me to do your will, for you are my God; may your good Spirit lead me on level ground" (Ps. 143:10). Choose to turn your anger into something beautiful so you can move along the path he chose for you even before time began.

I'm confused about where my husband is. I've always thought that when we die we go to be with the Lord. My next-door neighbor tells me that her church teaches after death we sleep until the day of

resurrection. I don't want to argue with her, but who is right?

The only source for a final answer to this question is the word of God. Paul cautions, "Don't have anything to do with foolish and stupid arguments" (2 Tim. 2:23).

The Bible says that, "The Lord himself will come down from heaven, with a loud command, with the voice of the archangel and with the trumpet call of God, and the dead in Christ will rise first" (1 Thess. 4:16). This verse refers to the time of the Second Coming of the Lord. Without getting into a foolish argument as to when that day will come, we can agree that it will occur. From this verse, some may infer that the dead won't rise until that day. This is also supported by the words, "Listen, I tell you a mystery: We will not all sleep, but we will all be changed—in a flash, in the twinkling of an eye, at the last trumpet. For the trumpet will sound, the dead will be raised imperishable, and we will be changed" (1 Cor. 15:51, 52).

There is a teaching that says when a person dies, their soul doesn't immediately go to an afterlife, but *sleeps* in the grave until the day of resurrection. This is known as *soul sleeping*. Some try to justify this doctrine by referring to Ecclesiastes 9:5, "For the living know that they will die, but the dead know nothing; they have no further reward, and even the memory of them is forgotten."

Others cite the account of the stoning of Stephen as recorded in Acts 7:59, 60, "While they were stoning him, Stephen prayed 'Lord Jesus, receive my spirit.' Then he fell on his knees and cried out, 'Lord, do not hold this sin against them.' When he had said this, he fell asleep."

But when we look at this passage we wonder how could Stephen fall asleep and still be in the grave when it's clear that Jesus had received his spirit. The expression "fell asleep" appears to be a gentler way of saying that a person died. It is a way of stating that the physical body has died.

You can understand this a little better if you think of the outer man and the inner man as defined in 2 Corinthians 4:16, "Though outwardly we are wasting away, yet inwardly we are being renewed day by day."

The outer man is the physical body, while the inner man is composed of soul and spirit. Death occurs when the inner man is separated from the outer man. At death the inner man (soul and spirit) goes immediately to the afterlife while the body *sleeps* until the resurrection.

The apostle Paul remarks in Philippians 1:21–24, " For to me, to live is Christ and to die is gain. If I am to go on living in the body, this will mean fruitful labor for me. Yet what shall I choose? I do not know! I am torn between the two: I desire to depart and be with Christ, which is better by far; but it is more necessary for you that I remain in the body."

In this passage, Paul is stating that when he dies it is gain for he goes to be with Christ, which he would prefer. If he believed in the concept of "soul sleeping," he would not have declared he would be with the Lord.

We're also told in Hebrews 12:1, 2 that those believers who have gone on before us form a sort of cheering section for us in heaven. "Since we are surrounded by such a great cloud of witnesses, let us throw off everything that hinders and the sin that so easily entangles, and let us run with perseverance the race marked out for us. Let us fix our eyes on Jesus, the author and perfecter of our faith." Does this not mean that those believers who preceded us in death are in the presence of God?

Read the words Jesus spoke to the repentant thief who was crucified along side of him. Jesus gave this man firm assurance the he was not going to sleep, "I tell you the truth, today you will be with me in paradise" (Luke 23:43). There can be no other explanation that upon his death the repentant thief went immediately into the presence of God.

Whatever your understanding is of what happens to a Christian at the time of death, just remember that our Abba Father is in total control of our life—both here and after death. He knows with perfect understanding what is best for each of us. In time we will know all. Until then, turn it all over to him and trust.

My life seems so useless now. My kids are grown and live out of town. They're busy with their own lives. I feel I'm in the way when I go to see them. I'm retired from my job. I feel there's no purpose to my life. Will I always feel this way?

When you've been widowed, it's very easy to throw a pity party for yourself. People all around you have their own wonderful life and there you are—a widow! Who needs you? You *are* useless.

There's a very easy answer to the question, "Who needs you?" The Lord God himself needs you. There's a story about a statue of Christ, which was damaged during the bombings of World War II. The hands on this statue were blown away. Someone purportedly put a sign on the statue to remind onlookers that Christ has no hands but ours.

Does that give you a clue as to who needs you? You're called to do the work he needs done in the world. All you need to do is look around and see the many opportunities you have to serve as Christ's hands. There are soup kitchens that need workers. Schools are always hoping for grandmothers to work with children who need some special attention. Hospitals need volunteers to help make patients' stays more pleasant. And these are only a few suggestions of the needs the Lord asks his people to fulfill.

You may say you're still grieving and can't possibly do anything that could be of help to another. James 4:9, 10 gives us insight into that. "Grieve, mourn and wail . . . Humble yourselves before the Lord, and he will lift you up." The Lord understands when you grieve. But when you truly seek the Lord's face and fall down before him, even in your sorrow, he promises he will lift you up—higher and higher.

So you see your life now is not useless—just different. You were needed in that marriage relationship. Now it's part of your past and you are needed in other areas. If those areas seem fuzzy or unfamiliar to you, ask the Lord specifically what he requires of you.

When you ask God fervently of what he wants you to do, he will lead you to high places. And when you're busy doing what he has called you to do, others will look at you in amazement. Then you will be doing as the Lord himself tells us to do: "Let your light shine before men ... and praise your Father in heaven" (Matt. 5:16).

I feel freer since my husband died. Does this really mean I'm glad he died?

A lot of widows feel a sense of being free. This may come as a result of watching their husbands go through a long, terminal illness. Now they are free from the anguish of a hopeless disease.

It may be a reaction to being single again after having been a married woman. When you were married there were always two people to consider. Now there's only one, you. Paul declares in Romans 7:2, "By law a married woman is bound to her husband as long as he is alive, but if her husband dies, she is released from the law of marriage." It's not that marriage should be thought of in the light of a rigid law, it's the tone of being married as opposed to not being married anymore. When you're released from those bonds of marriage, a sense of freedom can be the natural result. This does not necessarily mean that you're secretly (or overtly) glad that he died; it's just a reaction to what has happened. You're trying to make the best of the situation. Your life with your husband is now over.

"An unmarried woman ... is concerned about the Lord's affairs: Her aim is to be devoted to the Lord in both body and spirit" (1 Cor.7:34). You need to use this newly found freedom to determine where you can best serve in the kingdom of God. Perhaps there's a child who needs to learn about Jesus. Maybe there's a friend who desperately needs to talk to someone. Remember, your freedom now allows you to minister at all hours if need be. I'm sure that if you look around, you'll see a host of opportunities to serve the Lord and others now that you're single. The former things may be gone, but now you are called to new things.

Why does God allow suffering and death?

It may or may not comfort you to know that although this question has been asked many times for many years the answer to it remains an enigma. However, when you delve into the question of why a loving God allows suffering and death, you can find your faith deepened and your understanding of human nature sharpened.

The root lies in sin. God is not the source of evil. Far from it. He created a perfect world for us to live in. However, as you know, "Sin entered the world through one man" (Rom. 5:12). Since God's nature is perfect, he simply cannot tolerate sin. The result of of Adam and Eve's disobedience was an imperfect world in which we must live until Jesus comes again.

The imperfection of this world is exemplified in Luke 19:41, "As he [Jesus] approached Jerusalem and saw the city, he wept over it." Surely, our Savior grieves when he sees the suffering and death of his people.

But before you go pointing a figurative finger at Adam and Eve, you also need to look at yourself and realize how fragile and weak you really are, especially, when you try to contend with evil and sin on your own. When you realize this, the incarnation, death, and resurrection of the Son of God take on personal meaning for you.

You could choose to go on moaning and complaining about why there is suffering in the world. Or you could rest in the comfort the Lord offers. Sin and death were not God's choice for us, but because we're in this situation, he does offer grace to those who believe in him. For "where sin increased, grace increased all the more, so that, just as sin reigned in death, so also grace might reign through righteousness to bring eternal life through Jesus Christ our Lord" (Rom. 5:20, 21).

What a blessing that grace is! Undoubtedly, you appreciate grace all the more because of the trials, suffering, and setbacks that came your way in the valley of tears known as the world. The apostle Paul speaking of Jesus' words to him were, "My grace is sufficient for you, for my power is made perfect in weakness." And Paul's response was, "Therefore I will boast all the more gladly about my weaknesses, so that Christ's power may rest on me. That is why, for Christ's sake, I delight in weaknesses . . . in difficulties. For when I am weak, then I am strong." (2 Cor. 12:9, 10).

Pray that his perfect peace, through grace, settles on each of us.

I miss the sensual parts of my life with my husband. It's difficult to think of living the rest of my life like this. What can I do?

If you read secular self-help books on singleness, you could easily succumb to certain patterns of behavior. The world tells you that you're an adult. No one has the right to tell you what to do. If it feels good, do it. But the best self-help book is the Bible. In your seeking solace when you truly miss those sensual moments, the Bible offers insight into the path God chooses for you.

"You were bought at a price. Therefore honor God with your body" (1 Cor. 6:20). What does that mean? The price paid for you was the sacrificial death of the Son of God. Since the God of the Universe paid such a dear price for you, shouldn't you take those words to heart and keep your body pure for him?

You may then say, "But how can I possibly do this? Everywhere I look, the world is beckoning to me." It would be easy to give in, but every time you fend off those tempting feelings, you gain another victory. And in time, believe it or not, it does get easier.

I find the best way is to look for alternatives for meeting sensual needs—not in the same manner as when I was married, but using other sources. For example, I now take more time to care for my personal appearance. I have my nails done professionally. I go to the best salon that I can find to have my hair cut and colored.

Some widows treat themselves, from time to time, to body massages or aromatherapy. Bubble baths are an inexpensive way to get a sensual experience for a person who is sanctified and striving to be pure for the Lord. Think about it. Ask the Lord to show you how he wants you to deal with those sensual feelings that now must be subdued other ways.

"Blessed is the man (or woman) who perseveres under trial, because when he has stood the test, he will receive the crown of life that God has promised to those who love him" (James 1:12). Let us insert a resounding, "Blessed is the woman who perseveres" for the Lord has a special crown of life just waiting for those who truly seek to follow him.

Sometimes I feel guilty that I'm alive and my husband is dead. How can I resolve this?

"There is a time for everything, and a season for every activity under heaven; a time to be born and a time to die" (Eccles. 3:1, 2).

Are those words comforting to you or are they annoying? Your husband is no longer living. He is dead. When it is stated that way, it can be an extremely depressing thought. He's gone. He won't see his grandchildren grow up. He may have been so young when he died that he won't even see his own children grow up. His business is going on without him. This "time for everything" stuff just doesn't compute.

Intellectually you know that alive or dead, you are still in the hands of a loving God. "If we live, we live to the Lord; and if we die, we die to the Lord. So, whether we live or die, we belong to the Lord" (Rom. 14:8). But it still hurts.

And once you've worked your way through that "everything" stuff, you come to the realization that although your husband is no longer living, you are. This could make you feel guilty. So, rather than moping around and feeling guilty, look around and find reasons why the Lord has chosen to keep you here.

You can get a clue about this in the Scriptures. Paul says, "If I am to go on living in the body, this will mean fruitful labor for me" (Phil. 1:22). Paul struggled with a feeling of guilt and he, too, wondered why. He desired to be with the Lord Jesus, however, you can see from these words that he accepted his present status. So, for the time being, he would remain fruitful for the Lord. Use Paul as a model for your life.

My husband was my best friend and confidant. Now, I have no one to share my deepest thoughts with. My friends don't understand. Whom can I turn to?

I suppose that having your husband as your best friend is a blessing many other widows would have wished for in their marriages. But recognizing that still doesn't erase the yearning you now feel for what was and now is no more. You miss opportunities to bounce ideas off of him. You miss him as your companion. To put it simply, you miss him.

Now, with your best friend gone, what alternatives might you have? "There is a friend who sticks closer than a brother" (Prov. 18:24). And that best friend is the Lord himself.

I once heard of a woman who, when she prayed in her chair, would place another chair facing her. As she prayed she visualized seeing the Lord in that chair. They would have great conversations. No doubt, she asked him for advice or just told him of the events of her day.

In my experience, I find that I do talk less now that I'm a widow, which means that I learn more. It's been said that when you're talking you're not learning anything new. This is certainly true in my case. I've even been told that I'm a good listener. People tell me their problems all the time, and I just let them get it all out.

Perhaps the lack of talking with others can be replaced with the exceptionally good habit of praising the Lord. Consider this suggestion from the psalmist to "Sing to God, sing praise to his name, extol him who rides on the clouds— his name is the LORD—and rejoice before him. A father to the fatherless, a defender of the widows, is God in his holy dwelling" (Ps. 68:4, 5).

There you have it; praise causes rejoicing in our hearts . . . even in the hearts of widows. The Lord does indeed care that you're without your best friend. "Cast all your anxiety on him because he cares for you" (1 Pet. 5:7). He is there for you. He will be there for you. Trust him.

I get jealous when I see a woman who's not a widow. How can I overcome these feelings? Why are some women so lucky? Why did the Lord do this to me?

First of all, you need to establish that luck had nothing to do with the situation. The concept of luck is never used in the Bible. God remains in control.

The second fact is that jealousy is what the Old Testament calls coveting. One of the commandments given by God to the children of Israel was, "You shall not covet your neighbor's house. You shall not covet your neighbor's wife, or his manservant or maidservant, his ox or donkey, or anything that belongs to your neighbor" (Ex. 20:17). If feelings of envy creep into your life because someone else has her husband and you don't, you need to ask the Lord to help you overcome them. Proverbs 14:30 says that, "A heart at peace gives life to the body, but envy rots the bones." And who needs rotten bones?

As a widow, you do need peace. In seeking the Lord, you will find the contentment that you now lack. He gives perfect peace. So instead of being jealous and wishing for what you don't have, do as the apostle Paul did. "I have learned to be content whatever the circumstances. I know what it is to be in need, and I know what it is to have plenty. I have learned the secret of being content in any and every situation, whether well fed or hungry, whether living in plenty or in want. I can do everything through him who gives me strength" (Phil. 4:11–13). May that be your goal!

My husband put off getting his affairs in order and left me with a terrible mess of finances and legal entanglements. I'm angry with him for leaving me in this situation. What can I do?

First of all, "Get rid of all bitterness, rage and anger" (Eph. 4:31). Anger isn't helping the situation you're in. In fact, you're admonished to "Not let the sun go down while you are still angry, and do not give the devil a foothold" (Eph. 4:26, 27). In any marriage, except in unusual circumstances, one will be left alone. And being angry with the one who's gone may be an understandable human reaction. But look at the facts and realize your husband didn't choose to die. It's not part of an evil plot to put you in the predicament you're in today.

If you find yourself entangled in legal and financial problems, turn that anger into something positive by seeking solutions to the problems. The Bible warns that "plans fail for lack of counsel, but with many advisors they succeed" (Prov. 15:22).

You may need professional help, especially with the legal aspects of any problem. And note that the Bible suggests counselors (plural). You may find that speaking with several legal experts will yield the most effective composite advice. You may think that you can't do this alone. Find a trusted friend, son, daughter, or pastor to go with you. Each of you should take notes. Then, later, you can compare notes and discuss options. The final decision should still be yours, but a second opinion can help you clarify and sort out what you heard. In time you'll find yourself becoming stronger as you gain information about the situation.

Eventually, you *will* be able to say with confidence, "My decisions are right, because I am not alone. I stand with the Father" (John 8:16). Jesus spoke these words, but they can become a model for you as God's precious child. When you seek advice from counselors and ask the Lord to help in the confirmation of your plans, you will be prepared to continue into the future.

What are some pros and cons of going to live with one of my grown children?

This is a question I've wrestled with personally. Although I made a firm decision several years ago, there are still times when I think about the situation. My choice was to accept the invitation of my daughter and son-in-law to live with them. They had always said that would be the case, thinking it would not happen for years. But when the Lord chose to take my husband home at the age of 61, my daughter and son-in-law said, "Well, now you're with us."

In a sense they were following the commandment to "Honor your father and your mother, as the LORD your God has commanded you, so that you may live long and that it may go well with you in the land the LORD your God is giving you" (Deut. 5:16). But the reality goes deeper than that. They truly wanted me to leave my home and move in with them.

Leaving where I'd lived for so long was not as difficult as I'd thought, but leaving the friends I cherished was another matter. I still keep in touch and try to see them once in awhile, but it isn't always possible.

Putting two households together, even though there was one of me and four of them at the time, was a challenge. But with love, and much discussion we were able to work out many details. For one thing, I am not the official babysitter. My feeling is that I raised my children with no family nearby and no money for babysitting. So when my daughter works, the kids go to daycare. If there's an emergency, I try to find a way to help, but if I can't, then the parents have to work out a solution for themselves.

On the other hand, it was a blessing to be there with them when the third child was born. My daughter had some complications and needed several hospital stays after the birth. Everything worked smoothly for everyone, because I was there to help out with all the things the new mommy couldn't do.

Also, as the kids are growing and getting more and more homework, it is good to have three adults in the house to work with them. I find that my own children ask my advice more often as their children grow. In one sense I was following Paul's advice, "The older women . . . can train the younger women to love their husbands and children, to be self-controlled and pure, to be busy at home, to be kind, and to be subject to their husbands, so that no one will malign the word of God" (Titus 2:3–5)

Those words may sound lofty or archaic in today's culture, but the truths in them can be a model for how older people can bring insight in gentle ways to those with less experience.

Perhaps, after reading about the benefits of living with a grown child, you may still prefer to live alone. That's okay too. You're not really alone, you know. "The LORD watches over the alien and sustains the fatherless and the widow" (Ps. 146:9).

I just can't bring myself to dispose of his belongings. I feel disloyal, somehow, if I give away or dispose of any of his things. So, I closed the closet door and haven't done anything about it. Is this unrealistic?

Did you have a feeling that if you cleaned out his side of the closet he'd be upset that you had gotten rid of his things? If that's the case, you're not alone. Many widows have spoken of having had these same feelings. It's probably part of adjusting and accepting what really happened. So, rather than dealing with anymore pain, you should just refuse to give away his things, for now.

But if it's been six months or a year since his death and you still can't face getting rid of his things, you need to consider what might be happening. Perhaps you just can't put the former days in their proper perspective. "The old has gone, the new has come," we are told in 2 Corinthians 5:17. Holding on to your husband's belongings could mean that inwardly you're trying to hold on to him.

If that's true, you really need to concentrate on that verse from 2 Corinthians. The old has gone, but the new has come. Once again you're reminded, as a widow, that your former life is gone, but the Lord does have new things in store for you. Instead of clinging to the past, you're to look ahead to your new life. If you feel you still cling to the past, what concrete steps can you take to do something about it?

Resolve today to get rid of his belongings. The longer you put it off the more difficult it will be. I know that even opening the closet will bring back all those memories of what happened. Find a friend who will help you with decisions—and do it! You may think you can't do it, but with the Lord's help you'll be amazed at what you can do.

And once you've conquered your fear of getting rid of his things, you'll be ready to look for the new growth that will come, just as we're told in Proverbs 27:25, "The hay is removed and new growth appears and the grass from the hills is gathered in." Close your eyes right now and picture that field where the hay has been cut. What grows in its place? You are promised that new growth will appear. Picture in your mind the mown field, now ripe with lush, green grass—a symbol of the possibilities God has in store for you. Before you open your eyes, savor the look of the new grass in that field and thank the Lord for showing you what he's been eagerly waiting to do.

I was always the weaker person with illnesses and surgeries. My husband was the strong one. I never thought he would die first. Why did this happen?

To fully understand why this happened, you would need to understand the mind of God. And while you're here in this imperfect human body, you can never truly understand the "why" of anything. It's enough for us today to think about these words: "'For my thoughts are not your thoughts, neither are your ways my ways,' declares the LORD. 'As the heavens are higher than the earth, so are my ways higher than your ways and my thoughts than your thoughts'" (Isa. 55:8, 9).

I suppose you need to understand, in a limited way, that the reason the Lord chose to take your husband first is simply that he knows far better than you do what is best for all. He knows what must be done for his kingdom on earth. Your very existence is a part of this.

You may feel you can't do much for the Kingdom of God because you feel weak. The apostle Paul also considered himself to be weak, yet look at the good he was able to do, in spite of his weaknesses. "I will boast all the more gladly about my weaknesses, so that Christ's power may rest on me . . . I delight in weaknesses . . . in difficulties. For when I am weak, then I am strong" (2 Cor. 12:9, 10).

Paul knew his weaknesses, whatever they were; yet he trusted the Lord to give him strength for whatever task God had for him. The Lord has his reason for what happened. You may think you can't do it alone, but you are assured in Isaiah 41:10, "Do not fear, for I am with you; do not be dismayed,

146

for I am your God. I will strengthen you and help you; I will uphold you with my righteous right hand."

You are not in this alone. You may have lost your strong husband, but now you have a mighty God whose strength far exceeds that of any human. He's ready to give you the strength and stamina you need, so you can carry out the plan he has for you, "'For I know the plans I have for you,' declares the LORD, 'plans to prosper you and not to harm you, plans to give you hope and a future. Then you will call upon me and come and pray to me, and I will listen to you. You will seek me and find me when you seek me with all your heart'" (Jer. 29:11–13).

Even though I knew for months that my husband would die, when the moment came, I had such feelings of disbelief. Why is this?

While your husband was still alive, you still had hope that things would get better. After all, miracles do happen. You may have thought, *If I pray hard enough or if I have a prayer chain that circles the globe, my husband will recover.* You might have said to the Lord, "Do not let my hopes be dashed" (Ps. 119:116). But then one day it happened. Your husband died. Your hopes were dashed.

Even if your husband died suddenly or unexpectedly you may still have those feelings. And feelings of disbelief can come when the finality of death hits with such force. You had a marriage. You maintained hope for better things. And then it was over. No more would you see him. No more would you touch him. It was over.

You know there's a resurrection and you have that assurance that you will see him in heaven. "And this is the will of him who sent me, that I shall lose none of all that he has given me, but raise them up at the last day. For my Father's will is that everyone who looks to the Son and believes in him shall have eternal life, and I will raise him up at the last day" (John 6:39, 40). But it still hurts, and your emotions cling to what might have been. You are numb, shocked, and in disbelief.

By now you know that your time of disbelief was temporary. You may recall it from time to time. You may relive those moments over and over again. Just recognize that other widows have also gone through this. You're not alone in experiencing these feelings. In a way it can be thought of as a blessing from the Lord—a means of leading you gently into widowhood.

He's the one to cling to now. Tell him daily, "You have been my hope, O Sovereign LORD my confidence since my youth. From birth I have relied on you" (Ps. 71:5, 6). And then thank him for every feeling you have had or continue to have. He understands them all and is eager to comfort you.

I've met a man I feel I'm in love with. If I marry him I'll lose all my husband's pension benefits. So I'm seriously considering just living together. What's wrong with that? Doesn't the Lord understand today's economics?

Certainly, the Lord understands the economics of today. He understands the needs we all have, but he also knows that because of those needs, we can easily be led down paths he wouldn't choose for us. What looks tempting and reasonable in light of today's morals or economics is not necessarily the Lord's choice for you. "The wisdom of this world is foolishness in God's sight" (1 Cor. 3:19).

Begin by looking at two aspects of this possible live-in situation. The first centers on your sensual nature. Many modern psychologists claim it's alright to gratify your needs. They even say that if living together in an unmarried state satisfies that need, it's okay. But when you read the Word of God you see that his instructions give advice contrary to that of modern day psychologists:

"Do not use your freedom to indulge the sinful nature" (Gal.5:13).

"Put to death, therefore, whatever belongs to your earthly nature: sexual immorality, impurity, lust, evil desires and greed which is idolatry" (Col. 3:5).

"Clothe yourselves with the Lord Jesus Christ, and do not think about how to gratify the desires of the sinful nature" (Rom. 13:14).

The Lord furnished these guidelines for behavior because he loves us so deeply. He knows what is best for us, because he created us. As a Christian, you know how the Lord wants you to live, not only for your good, but for the good of others around you as well—your children, other Christians, and your unbelieving friends.

The second aspect of this question about living together deals with the potential loss of money if you choose to remarry. Do you suppose that the God who owns the cattle on a thousand hills would desert you when you strive to do what you know is right? "The LORD is good . . . He cares for those who trust in him" (Nah. 1:7).

The God of the universe does care about your finances. When you place your complete trust in him, he *will* provide for your needs. The Scriptures promise: "I provide water in the desert and streams in the wasteland, to give drink to my people, my chosen, the people I formed for myself that they may proclaim my praise" (Isa. 43:20, 21).

Turn your desires and your finances over to him and watch the wonders he will perform.

I feel so restless. I start projects and can't finish them. I think I'll do something and then I back out. I can't concentrate on anything. Where can I find contentment?

This is a very typical reaction of those who are widowed. It takes time to readjust to this new life. There are so many details needing attention and you're just getting used to the idea of being alone. You may feel a little like the writer of Ecclesiastes 2:11, "When I surveyed all that my hands had done and what I had toiled to achieve, everything was meaningless, a chasing after the wind; nothing was gained under the sun."

It sounds a little hopeless doesn't it? But take a deep breath and tell yourself these restless feelings won't last forever. Instead of chasing after the wind and exhausting yourself by doing everything at once, give yourself time. In other words, don't attempt to scale Mount Everest while you're still in the process of grieving and adjusting to this new status. Often, restlessness is the result of attempting too much or from staying too busy, so you don't have to think about your current situation.

If you find yourself darting about here and there and feeling restless, go to the source of peace and contentment—the Lord himself. "First seek the counsel of the LORD," you are told in 2 Chronicles 18:4. He can calm your sorrowful heart and help you learn to you put your trust in him. In Psalm 119:10, 11 you read, "I seek you with all my heart; do not let me stray from your commands. I have hidden your word in my heart." When you consistently seek the Lord, he *will* grant you incredible peace.

Holidays and special days were always a major part of our lives. How can I face them alone now?

The Lord has such a tender heart, and he cares that you're now facing holidays alone. If you question that, look at Proverbs 10:7: "The memory of the righteous will be a blessing." He understands that your special times are now going to be different. He is also eager to help you get through the them.

How does he do this?

First of all, look at the words of the parable told by Jesus in Luke 5:36. "No one tears a patch from a new garment and sews it on an old one. If he does, he will have torn the new garment, and the patch from the new will not match the old."

You may ask, "What does that verse have to do with my situation?" The Lord knows all about those special times you and your husband shared. But he's eager for you to start new traditions today without your husband. Maybe you could plan a special time with each of your grandchildren—just you and that child—beginning a new holiday or birthday tradition. Maybe you could do those things that no one else has time for: baking special cookies, stringing popcorn and cranberries for the Christmas tree, or decorating eggs for Easter. For birthday celebrations, you could make favors for each person, or bake a wonderful cake. Come up with your own ideas how to make new memories and traditions—not to replace what you had with your husband—but to make the future just as special.

With this beginning, keep reminding yourself that the Lord cares about your special memories. He knows that holidays and special occasions cause sorrow. Listen to the words of the psalmist, "I waited patiently for the LORD; he turned to me and heard my cry. He lifted me out of the slimy pit, out of the mud and mire; he set my feet on a rock and gave me a firm place to stand. He put a new song in my mouth, a hymn of praise to our God" (Ps. 40:1–3).

Every now and then I think I see him on the street, or at a store. Then I get so mad at myself when I realize that it can't be. Why do I imagine I see him? And why do I beat myself up for it?

First of all, you are not stupid for thinking you see him from time to time. Your husband was such a big part of your life that your innermost being is still getting used to fact that you can no longer see, feel, or touch him.

Instead of berating yourself for thinking you see him, take a deep breath, and reassure yourself that everything is under God's control, including those feelings you are having. He understands. His choice for you today is that you fix your eyes "not on what is seen, but on what is unseen. For what is seen is temporary, but what is unseen is eternal" (2 Cor. 4:18).

He knows how hard it is for you to let go of the past. He's not asking you to forget your husband. He just wants to lead you into another stage of life without him

The Lord knows that, sooner or later, you'll see a man who reminds you of your husband. You may think, *That man is wearing a shirt just like the one my husband used to wear.* When you trust the Lord to get you through these tough times, you are focusing your attention on things that truly matter— eternal things.

"Put on the new self, created to be like God in true righteousness and holiness" (Eph. 4:24) and seek the Lord's will. Don't look at the things of this world. Instead, do what Isaiah says, "Lift up your eyes to the heavens, look at the earth beneath; the heavens will vanish like smoke, the earth will wear out like a garment and its inhabitants die like flies. But my salvation will last forever, my righteousness will never fail" (Isa. 51:6). May those words be etched on your broken heart and comfort you now and for all eternity.